SOUTHERN
MY WAY

Simple Recipes, Fresh Flavors

GENA
KNOX

SOUTHERN MY WAY

Simple Recipes, Fresh Flavors

GENA KNOX

PHOTOGRAPHY BY ERICA GEORGE DINES

Published in the United States by Gena Knox Media, LLC, Athens, Georgia.
www.genaknox.com

Library of Congress Control Number: 2010931316

ISBN 978-0-615-37440-6

Printed in China

Designed by Gill Autrey/Gillican

First Edition

To my mother, a true Southern lady

GENA
KNOX

CONTENTS

Introduction

I GREW UP IN A TINY GEORGIA TOWN where farming shaped the landscape, the culture, and the community. Back then, there was no talk of slow food or locally sourced goods. Seasonal eating was a way of life. We didn't have farmer's markets—what we grew, we simply shared with friends and family. We'd bring a neighbor a basket of peaches from the orchards around our house and come home with a sack of plump tomatoes or purple hull peas, which as often as not would end up on the supper table that night.

From the time I was little, I loved helping out on my parents' farm, just a short distance from our house. I always looked forward to riding through town with my dad in his Grand Wagoneer to check on the crops after he got off work. Daddy would drive slowly along the edges of the fields, surveying the rows of peanuts, soybeans, and cotton and kicking up a thin veil of dust from the bone-dry earth.

When I was a teenager, my dad and one of his good friends, Mr. Buster, got the idea to plant a vegetable garden for their wives on our farm. That garden quickly sprawled into five acres of Silver Queen corn—more than enough for two families plus a crowd of friends. So Mr. Buster and my dad decided they had the perfect summer job for their two daughters (me and my friend Jacqueline): selling the extra ears to passersby.

With help from one of the farm workers, Jacqueline and I loaded my dad's old Chevy pickup with corn, drove into town, and parked right on the main square. It was at least 98 degrees outside, and between the heat and the gnats, we were miserable. At 12 ears for a dollar, we didn't make enough money to buy much, but that job managed to keep us busy and out of trouble for days.

My impromptu sales career didn't end there. Throughout the fall, we'd see Daddy's truck heading down the driveway, piled high with green peanuts. After he dumped them under our basketball goal, my friend Anne and I would sit for hours picking them off the vine. Fridays after school, my mom would boil a huge batch for us to stuff in brown paper bags, and on Saturdays, we'd set up a card table outside Anne's dad's Western Auto store, selling the peanuts for 50 cents a bag.

Much as I loved our farm and everything that we grew on it, I also felt an irresistible pull toward the kitchen. As soon as I could see over the countertop, I was expected to help get dinner on the table—a responsibility I actually looked forward to. Before I was old enough for a real summer job, my mom would leave me a list of tasks I could handle while she was at work: marinating chicken, snapping beans, slicing squash for a casserole.

Not only did all that prep work give me a crash course in kitchen basics, it also left me with a deep and abiding passion for farm-fresh goods at the height of their season. In those years we didn't think twice about it; the rhythms of rural living dictated much of what went on our plates. It wasn't until I'd gone to college and lived far from home that I understood how lucky I was to have come from such a strong tradition of kinship with the land.

This is the essence of my South, and I want to share it with you. I'm avid about seeking out foods from local farmers and artisans, some of whom you'll meet in this book—friends who, like me, believe in keeping our region's foodways and farming traditions vibrant. My recipes are rooted in the Southern classics I was raised on, but freshened with contemporary flavors, lightened up, and streamlined for busier lives.

Welcome, and I'm glad to have you along for this journey through the South I remember and the South I know today. I hope you'll come to love it as much as I do.

Gena Knox

Local, Fresh Flavors

I'VE ALWAYS FOUND a special satisfaction in putting foods on the table that were raised and nurtured by those I know personally. I look forward every year to biting into summer peaches from the orchards down the road from my childhood home, to shucking oysters from the boats of my favorite Florida oystermen, to grilling fall quail from my dad's south Georgia farm.

In this book, I introduce you to a handful of growers, artisans, and others who have dedicated themselves to keeping the foods of our region close to their roots. Whether they create handmade goat cheese or butcher beef from cattle fed on sweet Georgia grass, they feel as strongly as I do that these old-fashioned practices not only are essential to honoring our heritage, but also to building a culture of wholesome, flavorful, and sustainable eating.

I'm motivated in large part by the desire to feed my family food that's produced with integrity and without harmful additives or growing methods. But just as importantly, I think food tastes better when it's flavored by the soil and sea I've known since childhood, and when it holds a little bit of heart from those who nurture it, prepare it, and put it on the table. Simply put, it's like coming home.

GENA KNOX

STARTERS

Pickled Shrimp with Hearts of Palm

Zucchini and Mozzarella Crostini
with Basil Vinaigrette

Butterbean Bruschetta with Country Ham

Deviled Eggs, Bloody Mary-Style

Toasted Pecan Goat Cheese
with Tupelo Honey

Manchego-Stuffed Dates

Avocado Lime Dip

Cheese-Wrapped Olives

Onion Jam-Topped Crostini
with Bacon and White Cheddar Cheese

Spiced Ricotta-Stuffed Figs

Greek Meatballs with Goat Cheese Tzatziki Sauce

Oysters Rockefeller

Zucchini and Squash Icebox Pickles

Joanie's Toasted Pecans

Pickled Shrimp
with Hearts of Palm

Pickled shrimp are a staple of my cocktail parties, and I never have leftovers. This dish reminds me of the Masters Golf Tournament—there's always a bowl on the coffee table at my in-laws' home, for friends and family to nibble as they drop by en route to the course.

PREP TIME 20 minutes, plus chill time
COOK TIME 5 minutes
YIELDS 8 appetizer servings

1 pound large, unpeeled shrimp
1 tablespoon salt

Spices

½ teaspoon celery seed
1 teaspoon mustard seed
3 bay leaves
1 teaspoon black peppercorns
½ teaspoon red pepper flakes
½ teaspoon whole coriander

2 cloves garlic, thinly sliced
1 tablespoon capers
Zest and juice of 1 lemon
¾ cup white wine vinegar
¾ cup olive oil
1 lemon, thinly sliced
½ medium onion, preferably Vidalia,
  thinly sliced
1 (15-ounce) can hearts of palm, drained
  and sliced
1 (8- to 10-ounce) package frozen artichoke
  hearts, thawed and drained

FIRST Fill a large stockpot with water, season with 1 tablespoon salt, and bring to a boil. Add shrimp. Once water returns to a slight simmer, remove shrimp from heat, drain, and let cool (shrimp will be pink but not overcooked). Peel shrimp, leaving tails intact; set aside.

NEXT In a medium bowl, combine spices, garlic, capers, lemon zest, juice, vinegar, and oil. Season with salt and freshly ground black pepper and set aside. Place shrimp in a large non-reactive bowl (such as glass). Top with lemon slices, onions, hearts of palm, and artichoke hearts and drizzle with dressing. Gently toss with hands until ingredients are combined.

LAST Cover and refrigerate for at least 4 hours or up to 8 hours, occasionally tossing to coat shrimp in dressing.

Zucchini and Mozzarella Crostini
with Basil Vinaigrette

Summer farmer's markets are loaded with zucchini and, of course, fresh basil. What better way to enjoy these than with fresh mozzarella and a nice glass of wine?

PREP TIME 10 minutes
YIELDS 8 servings

Basil Vinaigrette

1 large bunch fresh basil (about 2 cups loosely packed leaves)
1 medium shallot, coarsely chopped
2 tablespoons white balsamic vinegar
1 tablespoon water
½ teaspoon cane sugar or honey
¼ teaspoon salt
5 tablespoons good-quality extra-virgin olive oil

Crostini

1 medium zucchini
2 teaspoons olive oil
1 teaspoon lemon juice
1 (4-ounce) ball fresh, water-packed mozzarella cheese
8 (½-inch-thick) baguette slices, cut at an angle and lightly toasted

FIRST To make dressing, puree basil, shallot, vinegar, water, sugar, and salt in a blender, stopping as needed to scrape down sides with a rubber scraper. With motor running, slowly pour in olive oil and puree until smooth. Season with freshly cracked black pepper to taste.

NEXT Using a vegetable peeler, slice zucchini into thin ribbons and gently toss with olive oil, lemon juice, and a pinch of salt.

LAST Arrange crostini on a platter and curl zucchini ribbons on top. Tear mozzarella into pieces and divide among crostini. Drizzle with vinaigrette and sprinkle with freshly cracked black pepper to serve.

Butterbean Bruschetta
with Country Ham

I can remember my Grandmama Peggy coming over and putting a big bowl of butterbeans in her lap to shell while she sat and visited with us. I never appreciated the hard work she put into shelling until later in life, when I started cooking butterbeans on my own.

PREP TIME 10 minutes
COOK TIME 15 minutes
YIELDS 12 servings

Crostini

1 fresh baguette, cut into 24 slices
   on the diagonal
Olive oil, plus more to serve
12 very thin slices country ham or prosciutto,
    torn in half

Butterbean puree

3 cups chicken or vegetable stock
2 cups fresh or frozen butterbeans
1 clove garlic, roughly chopped
1 tablespoon lemon juice
3 tablespoons olive oil

FIRST Preheat oven to 350°F. Lightly drizzle baguette slices with olive oil and toast in oven until slightly brown. Bring stock to a boil in a stockpot over medium-high heat. Add butterbeans and simmer until tender, about 8 minutes.

NEXT Drain butterbeans, reserving ½ cup cooking liquid, and place in food processor fitted with blade attachment; add garlic and lemon juice. While processing, slowly add olive oil; process until smooth. Add enough cooking liquid to reach desired consistency. Season with salt and pepper and set aside.

LAST Spread butterbean puree onto each baguette slice, top with ham, and drizzle with olive oil to serve.

Deviled Eggs, Bloody Mary-Style

Bloody Marys and deviled eggs are natural brunch partners, so it makes perfect sense to combine them into one delicious dish.

PREP TIME 15 minutes
COOK TIME 10 minutes
YIELDS 12 eggs

6   fresh eggs
3   tablespoons regular or light mayonnaise
1   tablespoon finely chopped celery
2   teaspoons horseradish
1 ½ tablespoons chopped, oil-packed
     sun-dried tomatoes
½   teaspoon Worcestershire sauce
½   teaspoon celery salt
Tabasco sauce to taste
½   cup sliced pimento-stuffed green olives
     for garnish

FIRST Place eggs in stockpot and add enough water to cover 1 inch above them. Bring water to a boil, remove from heat, cover, and let sit for 10 minutes. Remove eggs and plunge in ice water to cool. Peel, cut in half, and remove yolks, leaving whites intact. Place yolks in a mixing bowl.

NEXT Using the back of a fork, mash yolks with mayonnaise until combined. Stir in celery, horseradish, tomatoes, Worcestershire, celery salt, and Tabasco. Season to taste with black pepper.

LAST Mound yolk mixture in each egg white and garnish with olive slices.

Toasted Pecan Goat Cheese
with Tupelo Honey

Local goat cheese, rolled in Georgia pecans and paired with tupelo honey, creates a beautiful appetizer that is simple to prepare and can be made in advance.

PREP TIME 5 minutes
COOK TIME 10 minutes
YIELDS 8-10 servings

1 (11-ounce) log goat cheese, softened
¾ cup pecan halves
½ teaspoon salt
3 tablespoons tupelo honey
Fresh baguette, sliced for serving

FIRST Preheat oven to 325°F. Cut goat cheese log in half. Using hands, shape each half into a round disk and place on parchment paper.

NEXT Place pecans on baking sheet and sprinkle with ½ teaspoon salt. Toast until lightly browned, stirring occasionally, about 8 to 10 minutes. Remove pecans from oven and transfer to wax paper to cool. Once cooled, finely chop in a food processor or by hand. Roll each goat cheese round in pecans until coated on all sides, pressing pecans into cheese as needed. Refrigerate until ready to serve.

LAST Place goat cheese on serving dish, drizzle with honey, and serve with baguette slices. Soften goat cheese at room temperature before serving.

> **FROM MY KITCHEN** *The South is home to several award-winning cheesemakers—Fromagerie Belle Chèvre of Elkmont, Alabama and Sweet Grass Dairy of Thomasville, Georgia are two of my favorites. Artisan cheesemakers are popping up all around the country, so it's worth seeking out one near you.*

Manchego-Stuffed Dates

These little canapés are served at Five and Ten, my favorite restaurant in Athens. They remind me of the bacon-wrapped dates my grandmother used to serve at Christmas: a little sweet, a little salty, and totally irresistible.

PREP TIME 20 minutes
YIELDS 12 canapés

½ cup celery, very thinly sliced at an angle
½ teaspoon sherry vinegar
½ teaspoon olive oil, plus more for drizzling
12 Medjool dates
1 ounce Manchego cheese, cut into
   1-inch matchsticks
½ teaspoon smoked or regular paprika

FIRST In a small bowl, toss celery with vinegar and oil and lightly season with salt.

NEXT Gently cut a slit into each date using a small knife. Remove pit and stuff each date with 2 slices of celery and 1 stick of Manchego cheese.

LAST Arrange dates on a platter and drizzle lightly with olive oil. Sprinkle with just enough paprika to give the plate a little color, and serve.

Avocado Lime Dip

This creamy, citrus-spiked dip is great for dunking crudité or sturdy chips, or for spreading on a sandwich. I also love it with fresh boiled shrimp in the summertime.

PREP TIME 5 minutes
YIELDS 1 ½ cups

1   ripe avocado, peeled and seeded
½ cup plain yogurt (not Greek)
1   scallion, roughly chopped
2   tablespoons lime juice
¼ teaspoon salt

FIRST In a food processor or blender, puree avocado, yogurt, scallion, lime juice, and salt until smooth.

LAST Serve with vegetables or pita chips.

Cheese-Wrapped Olives

Very seldom will you arrive at a cocktail party in the South and not be offered a homemade cheese straw. The dough is extremely versatile; my mom favors it as a crispy coating for olives. One bite and you'll understand why.

PREP TIME 20 minutes
COOK TIME 15 minutes
YIELDS about 40 olives

1   (10-ounce) block sharp cheddar cheese, room temperature
1   stick (½ cup) unsalted butter, softened
1 ½ cups all-purpose flour
1 ½ teaspoons kosher salt
½   teaspoon cayenne pepper or more to taste
About 40 large, pimento-stuffed green olives

FIRST Preheat oven to 350°F. Shred cheese using a hand grater or a food processor with cheese-shredding attachment. Combine cheese, butter, flour, salt, and pepper in a food processor fitted with the blade attachment. Process until dough forms a ball and separates from side of processor.

NEXT Using hands, roll dough into 1-inch balls and shape 1 ball around each olive, making sure olive is completely covered in dough. Place on ungreased baking sheet about 2 inches apart.

LAST Bake for 15 minutes until lightly browned. Allow to cool before serving.

Onion Jam-Topped Crostini
with Bacon and White Cheddar Cheese

This sweet-salty jam marries beautifully with white cheddar cheese. I also use it to embellish grilled meats such as lamb.

PREP TIME 10 minutes
COOK TIME 20 minutes
YIELDS 12 crostini

2   teaspoons olive oil
1   slice bacon, chopped
1   medium Vidalia or other sweet onion, thinly sliced
1   medium red onion, thinly sliced
3   tablespoons brown sugar
½   teaspoon fresh rosemary
¼   teaspoon salt
1   tablespoon good-quality bourbon

12 (½-inch-thick) baguette slices, cut on an angle and lightly toasted
12 (¼-inch-thick) slices white cheddar cheese
1   tablespoon roughly chopped flat-leaf parsley

FIRST In a large skillet, heat oil over medium heat. Add bacon and cook for 30 seconds. Add onions and cook, stirring frequently, until they begin to soften, about 8 minutes. Stir in sugar, rosemary, and salt; continue cooking for 10 minutes or until onions are golden and very tender. Stir in bourbon and season with freshly cracked pepper.

NEXT Preheat oven to 450°F. Arrange toasted baguette slices on a baking sheet and top each with 1 slice of cheese. Bake for 3 minutes or until cheese is melted and bubbly.

LAST Spoon jam atop crostini, garnish with parsley, and serve.

Spiced Ricotta-Stuffed Figs

Right around mid-July, Georgia figs are at their ripest, and a single tree can yield so many at once that you have to make quick use of them. This easy appetizer is one of my favorites. You can also stuff the figs with goat, blue, or feta cheese.

PREP TIME 15 minutes
COOK TIME 10 minutes
YIELDS 4 servings

8   medium figs
½   cup part-skim ricotta cheese
2   tablespoons chopped walnuts
4   teaspoons honey, divided
¼   teaspoon ground cinnamon
⅛   teaspoon ground nutmeg
⅛   teaspoon salt
4   slices prosciutto, cut in half lengthwise
8   (½-inch-thick) baguette slices (optional)

FIRST Preheat oven to 350°F. Slice figs from top to bottom into quarters, without cutting all the way through, and set aside.

LAST Combine cheese, walnuts, 2 teaspoons honey, cinnamon, nutmeg, and salt. Gently spoon mixture into each fig. Wrap 1 prosciutto slice around each fig to hold together; arrange on a greased baking sheet and bake for 10 minutes or until figs are heated through. Drizzle with remaining honey and serve with baguette slices, if desired.

> **FROM MY KITCHEN** *If you are short on time, slice figs into halves or quarters and roast for 8 to 10 minutes. Spread ricotta mixture on toasted baguette slices, top with figs, and drizzle with honey before serving.*

Greek Meatballs
with Goat Cheese Tzatziki Sauce

Our good friend Tasia Malakasis, owner of Fromagerie Belle Chèvre and a fabulous cook and host, has such unique ways of using her delicious cheese. She served us these meatballs, with her take on classic tzatziki sauce, at her home in Huntsville, Alabama.

PREP TIME 20 minutes
COOK TIME 8 minutes
YIELDS 30 meatballs

Sauce

6   ounces Greek yogurt
1 ½ ounces fresh goat cheese, softened
½   cup diced English cucumber
¼   cup fresh lemon juice
2   tablespoons chopped fresh dill
1   small clove garlic
¼   teaspoon kosher salt

Meatballs

1   pound ground sirloin or bison
1   egg
¼   cup dried bread crumbs
¼   cup fresh mint, chopped
2   tablespoons finely chopped red onion
1   tablespoon finely chopped scallions
¼   teaspoon kosher salt

FIRST Preheat oven to broil. Combine sauce ingredients in a blender or food processor and pulse until well blended. Season with freshly ground black pepper to taste and refrigerate until ready to serve.

NEXT In a bowl, combine sirloin, egg, bread crumbs, mint, onion, scallions, and salt; season with freshly ground black pepper to taste. Using hands, mix gently and form into 1 ½-inch balls. Place meatballs on a wire rack set on top of a baking sheet.

LAST Broil meatballs for about 8 minutes or until done. Serve with sauce for dipping.

FROM MY KITCHEN *For a main course, toss cooked couscous with fresh mint, lemon juice, and olive oil, top with meatballs, and serve with Goat Cheese Tzatziki Sauce. The sauce is a perfect accompaniment to salmon as well.*

Oysters Rockefeller

Every Thanksgiving, my dad buys a bushel of Apalachicola oysters. We devour them raw with Bloody Marys but also save a few to roast Rockefeller-style. There are a hundred different versions of this dish, but of course my mom's is my favorite.

PREP TIME 10 minutes
COOK TIME 20 minutes
YIELDS 12 oysters

12 fresh oysters on the half shell
3 cups kosher or rock salt

4 tablespoons butter
¼ cup plus 1 tablespoon chopped scallions
4 cups chopped fresh spinach
¼ cup all-purpose flour
½ cup white wine
2 tablespoons lemon juice
½ teaspoon salt
½ cup finely grated, good-quality Parmesan cheese
⅓ cup fresh bread crumbs

Lemon wedges for serving

FIRST Preheat oven to 400°F. Spread salt in rimmed baking sheet and nestle oysters into the bed of salt.

NEXT Melt butter in a medium saucepan over medium heat. Add scallions and sauté 1 minute until soft. Add spinach and cook until wilted. Stir in flour until mixture forms a roux (thick paste). Add wine and lemon juice and continue stirring until it forms a cream sauce too thick to pour. Season with salt and freshly cracked pepper.

LAST Top each oyster with a heaping tablespoon of spinach mixture. Sprinkle with cheese, then bread crumbs. Place pan on middle rack of oven and bake for 15 minutes or until topping is bubbly and bread crumbs are browned. Serve with lemon wedges.

Zucchini and Squash Icebox Pickles

Zucchini and squash are notorious for overwhelming gardeners (and their neighbors) with prolific yields. Here's one solution for staying on top of them. Pair these pickles with sandwiches or serve them with good cheese as a starter.

PREP TIME 15 minutes, plus chill time
COOK TIME 8 minutes
YIELDS 1 quart

2   medium zucchini, thinly sliced
2   medium crookneck squash, thinly sliced
1   small onion, thinly sliced
1   tablespoon salt
¾   cup apple cider vinegar
¾   cup white wine vinegar
¾   cup sugar
2   cloves garlic, thinly sliced
1   teaspoon mustard seed
1   teaspoon dill seed
½   teaspoon red pepper flakes

Special equipment: 1-quart mason jar

FIRST Toss vegetables and salt in a large bowl to coat. Place vegetables in colander set over a bowl and refrigerate for 8 hours or overnight. Rinse and drain vegetables and spoon into a 1-quart mason jar.

NEXT In a medium saucepan over medium-high heat, combine vinegars, sugar, garlic, mustard, dill, and red pepper flakes. Stir to dissolve sugar, bring to a boil, and reduce heat to simmer. Cook for 8 minutes or until slightly thickened.

LAST Pour vinegar mixture over vegetables, seal jar, and let cool. Store in refrigerator for up to 1 week.

Joanie's Toasted Pecans

Every time I smell these roasting in the oven, I vividly remember my parents' dinner parties: bowls of pecans and cheese straws at the bar and Willie Nelson on the record player.

PREP TIME 5 minutes
COOK TIME 35 minutes
YIELDS about 4 cups

4   tablespoons unsalted butter, melted
3   tablespoons Worcestershire sauce
1   teaspoon kosher salt
¼   teaspoon cayenne pepper or more to taste
1   pound pecan halves

FIRST Preheat oven to 300°F. Combine melted butter, Worcestershire sauce, salt, and pepper in a small bowl. Pour over pecans and toss to coat.

NEXT Spread pecans on a rimmed baking sheet in a single layer.

LAST Roast on middle rack of oven for 30 to 35 minutes, stirring every 10 minutes, until pecans are toasted light brown. Remove from oven and spread pecans on wax paper to cool. Store at room temperature.

Savannah Bee Company

SAVANNAH, GA Ted Dennard's passion for honeybees lies at the soul of Savannah Bee Company, an enterprise that began in his kitchen and today bottles some of the purest and most delicious honey in the region. A longtime beekeeper, Dennard is as enthusiastic about honey's health benefits as he is about its vibrant, complex flavors. Among his company's standout products are the specialty honeys that are flavored by a single type of flora, including Southern classics such as tupelo.

Left: Ted Dennard, the founder of Savannah Bee Company, holds honeycomb fresh from the hive. Savannah Bee offers a line of everyday and specialty honeys, honeycomb, products made with natural beeswax, and more.

Dennard welcomes guests to the Savannah Bee Company retail shop in Savannah, Georgia.

SOUPS

Greek Summer Gazpacho

**Sweet Corn Chowder
with Basil and Crumbled Bacon**

Asparagus Soup with Lemon Cream

Summer Squash and Buttermilk Soup

Sherried Wild Mushroom Soup

Vidalia Onion Soup

Rustic Tomato and Bread Soup

Roasted Cauliflower Soup

Butternut Squash and Apple Soup
with Molasses-Glazed Pecans

Greek Summer Gazpacho

This recipe is ideal when tomatoes are at their peak. Gazpacho was a summertime staple at our house when I was growing up, but I've put a spin on my mom's recipe with a few of my favorite Mediterranean flavors. I think it tastes best when the texture is on the chunky side, so take care not to process the vegetables into a puree.

PREP TIME 20 minutes, plus chill time
YIELDS 8-10 servings

3 large, ripe tomatoes, cored
1 English cucumber
1 yellow bell pepper, cored and seeded
1 small sweet onion
2 cloves garlic
½ cup Kalamata olives, pitted
¼ cup loosely packed fresh oregano leaves
½ cup loosely packed fresh mint leaves
¼ cup red wine vinegar
5 cups organic tomato juice
6 ounces feta cheese, cubed

FIRST Roughly chop tomatoes, cucumber, pepper, onion, and garlic and place in a food processor. Pulse until slightly chunky (do not over-process). Transfer to a large bowl.

NEXT Add olives, oregano, mint, and vinegar to processor and pulse until slightly chunky (or desired consistency). Add olive mixture to tomato mixture, stir in juice, and season with salt and pepper to taste.

LAST Refrigerate for at least 4 hours or overnight. Stir in cubed feta just before serving.

FROM MY KITCHEN *English cucumbers, which you'll often find wrapped in plastic, have a mild, sweet flavor. Because they lack the thick, waxy skin that regular cucumbers have, they don't need to be peeled.*

Sweet Corn Chowder
with Basil and Crumbled Bacon

This soup transports me straight back to my childhood days selling just-picked Silver Queen corn from my parents' farm. It takes time to cut corn off the cob, but the sweet, juicy payoff is worth every minute.

PREP TIME 20 minutes
COOK TIME 1 hour 10 minutes
YIELDS 4 servings

6   ears sweet corn, shucked
2   teaspoons olive oil
1   medium Vidalia or other sweet onion, chopped
¼   cup chopped celery
1   bay leaf
½   teaspoon chopped fresh rosemary
1   teaspoon chopped fresh thyme (½ teaspoon dried)
4   large basil leaves
Cayenne pepper to taste
2   slices cooked bacon

FIRST Using a sharp knife, cut corn off cobs and set aside. You should have about 5 cups of corn. Place cobs in large stockpot and cover with 8 cups of water. Bring to a boil, reduce heat, and simmer for 35 minutes.

NEXT While stock is simmering, heat oil in a stockpot over medium heat. Add onion, celery, and bay leaf and sauté for about 4 minutes until softened but not brown. Add corn, rosemary, and thyme and continue cooking about 3 minutes. Remove corncobs from stock and add 4 cups stock to corn mixture. Bring to a boil, reduce heat, and let simmer with lid off for 30 minutes.

LAST Remove soup from heat, discarding bay leaf, and let cool slightly. In a blender, puree about ¾ of the soup and the basil leaves, working in batches if necessary. Return to pot to reheat and season with salt and cayenne pepper to taste. Spoon into four bowls and garnish with crumbled bacon.

Asparagus Soup with Lemon Cream

This simple soup incorporates all my favorite spring flavors: Vidalia onions, mint, and lemon.

PREP TIME 10 minutes
COOK TIME 15 minutes
YIELDS 6 servings

Soup

1   tablespoon butter
¾   cup finely chopped shallots
1   celery rib, chopped
2   pounds thin asparagus (2 bunches)
2 ½ cups vegetable or chicken stock
1   tablespoon fresh lemon juice
¼   teaspoon cayenne pepper or to taste
2   tablespoons mint, finely chopped
1   cup milk

Lemon Cream

½   cup sour cream
2   teaspoons lemon juice
½   teaspoon lemon zest

FIRST Heat butter in a large saucepan over medium heat. Add shallots and celery and sauté until tender, about 5 minutes. Add asparagus and a pinch of salt and sauté for an additional 3 minutes or until asparagus is bright green.

NEXT Add stock and simmer until asparagus is tender, about 5 minutes. Add lemon juice, cayenne, and mint. Working in batches, puree soup with a blender, or use a soup emulsifier. Add enough milk to reach desired consistency, and season to taste with salt and pepper.

LAST In a small bowl, combine sour cream, lemon juice, and zest. Ladle soup into 6 bowls and top each with a dollop of lemon cream. Drizzle with olive oil if desired.

Summer Squash and Buttermilk Soup

When our garden was brimming with summer squash, my mom would steam them with onions as a side dish for Sunday lunch. I've turned her recipe into an herb-scented soup, with tangy buttermilk to cut the sweetness of the squash.

PREP TIME 15 minutes
COOK TIME 25 minutes
YIELDS 6 servings

1 tablespoon unsalted butter
1 medium Vidalia or other sweet onion, chopped
2 pounds crookneck squash, sliced into half-moons
2 cups chicken or vegetable stock
1 teaspoon salt
1 ½ teaspoons chopped fresh thyme
1 ½ teaspoons chopped fresh chives
½ cup buttermilk
Fruity olive oil for drizzling

FIRST Melt butter in a medium saucepan over medium heat. Add onion and sauté until soft but not brown, about 5 minutes. Add squash and cook, stirring often, for an additional 5 minutes.

NEXT Add stock and salt. Bring to a boil, reduce heat, and simmer for 10 minutes or until squash are tender. Stir in herbs, remove from heat, and let cool slightly. Using a blender or soup emulsifier, and working in batches if needed, puree soup until smooth.

LAST Return soup to pot to reheat. Stir in buttermilk, adding additional stock or buttermilk if texture is too thick. To serve, ladle soup into bowls and drizzle lightly with olive oil.

Sherried Wild Mushroom Soup

Sherry appears often in many old Southern cookbooks, but I don't come across it as much in modern-day recipes. It adds a nice finish to many dishes; just be sure to use real sherry and not the cooking sherry found in grocery stores.

PREP TIME 20 minutes
COOK TIME 40 minutes
YIELDS 6 servings

1   tablespoon butter, divided
2   leeks, white and light green parts only, halved and thinly sliced (about 2 cups)
8   ounces assorted wild mushrooms, such as portobello or cremini
3   ounces shiitake mushrooms, stems removed
3   tablespoons flour
½   cup white wine
2 ½ cups mushroom stock
2   teaspoons fresh thyme
½   teaspoon dry mustard
½   teaspoon salt
1   cup 1 percent milk
¼   cup half-and-half
3   tablespoons dry sherry
1   tablespoon chopped fresh parsley

FIRST Melt ½ tablespoon butter in a large stockpot over medium heat. Add leeks and sauté for 10 minutes, until softened. Add remaining butter and mushrooms; sauté until browned and tender, about 8 minutes.

NEXT Add flour and stir to incorporate. Stir in wine, stock, thyme, mustard, and salt. Bring soup to a boil, reduce heat, and simmer for 15 minutes. Reduce heat to a low simmer; add milk, half-and-half, and sherry. Simmer for an additional 5 minutes.

LAST Season with additional salt, if needed, and freshly cracked pepper. Garnish with chopped parsley and serve.

FROM MY KITCHEN *Mushroom stock can be found among organic soups in most grocery stores. You can substitute organic beef broth if necessary.*

Vidalia Onion Soup

Spring's Vidalia onions have a mild, sweet flavor that mellows this decadent onion soup. Although it takes some time to cook, it is quite easy to prepare and fills the house with a delicious aroma as it simmers on the stove.

PREP TIME 20 minutes
COOK TIME 1 hour 10 minutes
YIELDS 4 servings

1 ½ tablespoons butter
2 pounds Vidalia or other sweet onions, halved and thinly sliced
2 tablespoons brown sugar
1 teaspoon salt
2 teaspoons chopped fresh thyme
1 bay leaf
2 tablespoons all-purpose flour
½ cup sherry
¾ cup red wine
4 cups organic beef stock

4 (½-inch-thick) baguette slices, cut on an angle and toasted
4 ounces thinly sliced Gruyère cheese

FIRST Melt butter in a large stockpot over medium heat. Add onions, sugar, salt, thyme, and bay leaf; sauté for 40 minutes until onions are golden brown and caramelized. Sprinkle flour over onions and stir until combined. Add sherry and wine, stirring to scrape up brown bits from bottom of pan, and simmer for about 3 minutes. Stir in stock, bring to a light simmer, and cook for 30 minutes. Remove bay leaf and season soup with salt and pepper to taste.

LAST Ladle soup into 4 ovenproof bowls. Top each with 1 bread slice and ¼ cheese. Place bowls on a baking sheet and broil for 2 to 3 minutes until cheese melts and begins to brown.

FROM MY KITCHEN *As an alternative to Gruyère, Thomasville Tomme cheese from Georgia's Sweet Grass Dairy is fabulous with this soup.*

Rustic Tomato and Bread Soup

Tomatoes and basil might be my all-time favorite combination of flavors. This soup tastes like summer, but thanks to good-quality canned tomatoes, you can make it all year round.

PREP TIME 15 minutes
COOK TIME 35 minutes
YIELDS 6 servings

1   cup cherry or grape tomatoes
1 ½ tablespoons extra-virgin olive oil, divided
4   cloves garlic, chopped, divided
1   large bunch fresh basil (about 2 cups loosely packed leaves), divided
1   (28-ounce) can whole tomatoes, preferably organic
5   slices good-quality bread, cut into 1-inch cubes (about 2 cups)
   Freshly grated Pecorino cheese for garnish

FIRST Preheat oven to 350°F. Toss cherry tomatoes with 1 tablespoon olive oil, 1 clove chopped garlic, and ½ cup basil leaves. Spread on an oiled baking pan and roast for about 20 minutes or until tomatoes begin to burst.

NEXT While tomatoes are roasting, heat ½ tablespoon olive oil in a large pot over medium heat. Sauté remaining garlic and basil leaves until leaves are wilted, about 30 seconds. Add canned tomatoes, breaking up with back of spoon. Stir in 3 ½ cups water. Bring to a boil, reduce heat, and simmer for 15 minutes.

LAST Stir in roasted tomatoes and bread. Season to taste with salt and pepper; top with cheese to serve.

FROM MY KITCHEN *Use good-quality white bread, such as ciabatta or a Tuscan loaf, for this recipe; do not use sandwich bread or whole-wheat bread.*

Roasted Cauliflower Soup

The roasted garlic is subtle in this soup, allowing the richness of the browned cauliflower to shine through. It's a nice starter to any cold-weather meal.

PREP TIME 10 minutes
COOK TIME 30 minutes
YIELDS 4 servings

1   (2-pound) head cauliflower, cut into florets
4   cloves garlic, unpeeled
1   tablespoon olive oil
½   teaspoon salt
4   cups chicken or vegetable stock
Parmesan cheese shavings and olive oil
    for garnish

FIRST Preheat oven to 450°F. Toss cauliflower with garlic, oil, and salt and spread on rimmed, lightly greased baking sheet. Roast cauliflower until tender and beginning to brown, about 18 minutes.

NEXT Remove garlic from pan, transfer cauliflower to a stockpot, and add stock. Gently peel skins from garlic and discard. Add peeled garlic cloves to soup. Bring to a boil, reduce heat, and simmer for 10 minutes. Puree soup with a soup emulsifier or, working in batches, in a blender. Return soup to pot over low heat and season with freshly ground pepper.

LAST Ladle soup into 4 bowls, drizzle with olive oil, and top with cracked pepper and cheese shavings.

Butternut Squash and Apple Soup
with Molasses-Glazed Pecans

Nothing says fall like butternut squash soup—my very favorite. Molasses gives the pecans a sweet crunch and earthy, mellow flavor.

PREP TIME 20 minutes
COOK TIME 50 minutes
YIELDS 4 servings

Soup

1   (2-pound) butternut squash
1 ½ tablespoons olive oil, divided
1   small onion, chopped (1 cup)
2   cloves garlic, minced
1   stalk celery, chopped
1   Golden Delicious apple, peeled, cored, and chopped
3   cups chicken or vegetable stock
1   cup apple cider
1   teaspoon salt
Sour cream to garnish

Pecans

½   cup pecans
2   tablespoons molasses
1   tablespoon sugar

FIRST Preheat oven to 350°F. Cut squash in half lengthwise and remove seeds with a spoon. Drizzle inside of squash with ½ tablespoon oil and sprinkle lightly with salt. Place, cut side down, on a foil-lined baking pan and bake for 20 minutes. Let cool, peel with vegetable peeler, and cut into 1-inch chunks.

NEXT Cook onion, garlic, celery, and apple in 1 tablespoon olive oil in large stockpot over medium heat, stirring frequently, until onion is softened, about 7 minutes. Add squash, stock, cider, and salt. Bring to a boil, reduce heat, and simmer, uncovered, for 20 minutes. Puree in blender, working in batches, or process with a soup emulsifier. Return to stove to reheat.

LAST To toast pecans, preheat oven to 350°F. In a medium bowl, toss pecans with molasses and sugar to coat. Spread pecans on a greased pan and toast in oven for 8 minutes. Transfer pecans to wax paper to cool, separating them with a spoon. Ladle soup into bowls and top each with a small spoonful of sour cream and pecans.

> **FROM MY KITCHEN** *Winter squash can be tough, so I usually pre-bake them before peeling and chopping, which makes the prep work much easier.*

Sweet Grass Dairy
Fromagerie Belle Chèvre

THOMASVILLE, GA • ELKMONT, AL Southerners are renowned for scores of food traditions, but cheese hasn't generally been one of them. Today, that's changing, thanks to small-scale artisan dairies such as Georgia's Sweet Grass Dairy, owned by Jessica and Jeremy Little, and Alabama's Fromagerie Belle Chèvre, owned by Tasia Malakasis. Their passion for handcrafted cheeses, made with natural milk from free-range herds, and the care that goes into their production comes through in every delicious bite.

*Left: In artisan cheeses from Sweet Grass Dairy, the pure, clean flavors of the grasses on which the animals graze are subtle yet discernible. **Above:** Playful as puppies, a few of the goats that produce the milk for Belle Chèvre's cheeses prance in their open pasture.*

Right: "*I love the fact that our cheeses are good enough to be sold in Dean & Deluca, but are also in the Piggly Wiggly in Elkmont, Alabama,*" says Tasia Malakasis (pictured) of Belle Chèvre.

SALADS

Georgia Caprese Salad with Lime Vinaigrette

Roasted Beet and Arugula Salad with Goat Cheese Ranch

Winter Grapefruit and Avocado Salad

Arugula Salad with Lemon Parmesan Vinaigrette

Baby Green and Fig Salad with Cane Syrup Vinaigrette

Spinach Salad with Strawberries and Blue Cheese

Green Jacket Salad

Five Easy Salad Dressings

Basil Oil

Georgia Caprese Salad
with Lime Vinaigrette

This Southern spin on an Italian classic screams summer. When it's made with fresh, local peaches, you can't top it.

PREP TIME 15 minutes
YIELDS 4 servings

Dressing

Juice and zest of 1 lime
1 tablespoon champagne or white wine vinegar
1 tablespoon water
1 tablespoon honey
½ teaspoon salt
¼ cup olive oil
2 tablespoons chopped fresh mint

Salad

2 (4-ounce) balls fresh, water-packed mozzarella cheese
4 ripe peaches, unpeeled, each cut into 8 wedges
½ cup fresh basil leaves

FIRST To prepare dressing, combine lime juice, zest, vinegar, water, honey, and salt. Slowly whisk in olive oil and set aside.

NEXT Cut cheese into 1-inch pieces and gently toss with peaches and basil leaves.

LAST Whisk mint into dressing and toss about 2 tablespoons (or more to taste) with salad. Season with freshly cracked pepper and serve.

Roasted Beet and Arugula Salad
with Goat Cheese Ranch

Who doesn't like ranch dressing? This classic is always a crowd-pleaser when I entertain. My homemade version adds fresh goat cheese for a velvety texture and bright, tangy top note.

PREP TIME 15 minutes
COOK TIME 30-40 minutes
YIELDS 6 servings

Salad

6   medium red or yellow beets
5   ounces baby arugula
¼   cup pistachios, shelled

Dressing

1 ½ ounces fresh goat cheese, softened
2   tablespoons mayonnaise
2   tablespoons minced scallions
1   tablespoon finely chopped chives
1   tablespoon white wine vinegar
1 ½ teaspoons minced red onion
¼   cup plus 2 tablespoons buttermilk

FIRST Preheat oven to 425°F. Trim greens from beet roots, leaving about 1 inch above the root. Scrub beets and wrap each in a 12-inch piece of foil. Place on a baking sheet and roast for 30 to 40 minutes, depending on size, until beets are tender when pierced with a knife. Loosen foil around beets and let cool.

NEXT Combine dressing ingredients in a blender and mix until smooth; season with salt and pepper to taste. Rub skins from beets, using a paring knife to remove tougher skin. Slice in half from stem to tip, lay flat, and cut into ¼-inch-thick slices.

LAST Arrange arugula and beets on large platter. Top with pistachios and drizzle with dressing.

> **FROM MY KITCHEN** *So many people assume they won't like beets (or perhaps never got beyond the canned kind), but they are as sweet as candy and pair beautifully with assertive greens such as arugula. They're also easy to grow; we plant them in our garden each year and look forward to crops of fresh beets in the fall and spring.*

Winter Grapefruit and Avocado Salad

With my hometown so close to Florida, boxes of fresh grapefruits and oranges always make popular Christmas gifts among family and friends. They're often used for ambrosia, but there's only so much of that you can eat. This refreshing salad makes a nice starter to a winter meal.

PREP TIME 10 minutes
YIELDS 4 servings

Salad

2   pink grapefruits
2   ripe but firm avocados
⅓   cup torn basil leaves
1   head buttercrunch lettuce, torn into large pieces

Dressing

2   tablespoons minced shallots
1   teaspoon soy sauce
1   teaspoon honey
½   teaspoon sesame oil
½   teaspoon minced fresh ginger
2   tablespoons olive oil

FIRST Peel and segment the grapefruits, reserving 4 tablespoons juice.

NEXT To prepare dressing, whisk together reserved grapefruit juice, shallots, soy, honey, sesame oil, ginger, and olive oil. Season with salt and freshly ground black pepper; set aside.

LAST Quarter avocados lengthwise and remove pit and peel. Cut lengthwise into ½-inch slices and place in a large bowl. Gently toss avocado, grapefruit segments, and basil with desired amount of dressing. Arrange lettuce on 4 salad plates, top with avocado mixture, and serve.

> **FROM MY KITCHEN** *With fresh, local shrimp or crab, this becomes a light but satisfying lunch. You can easily substitute orange segments for the grapefruit, if you like.*

Arugula Salad
with Lemon Parmesan Vinaigrette

This blend of peppery arugula and tart citrus—always a hit with family and friends—packs a lot of flavor with minimal effort. It's great to have in your repertoire for hurry-scurry weeknights, but elegant enough for a dinner party.

PREP TIME 5 minutes
YIELDS 4 servings

Dressing

Zest of ½ lemon
2 tablespoons fresh lemon juice
¼ teaspoon honey
¼ teaspoon salt
4 tablespoons olive oil
¼ cup finely grated, good-quality
    Parmesan cheese

Salad

6 cups baby arugula
1 avocado, thinly sliced

FIRST Whisk together lemon zest, juice, honey, salt, and olive oil. Add cheese, season with pepper, and whisk until well combined.

LAST In a large bowl, toss arugula and avocado with enough dressing to coat. Divide among 4 plates and serve. Store leftover dressing in refrigerator for up to 4 days.

Baby Green and Fig Salad
with Cane Syrup Vinaigrette

This is one of my favorite salads to serve during the fall and winter months. The cane syrup gives the dressing a full-bodied and distinctly Southern flavor, but you can substitute maple syrup.

PREP TIME 15 minutes
YIELDS 4 servings

Dressing

1 ½ tablespoons apple cider vinegar
1   tablespoon cane syrup or maple syrup
1   teaspoon Dijon mustard
¼   teaspoon salt
2   tablespoons olive oil

Salad

4   cups baby greens
2   pears, cut in half, cored, and thinly sliced
½   cup dried mission figs
¼   cup walnuts, lightly toasted

FIRST Combine vinegar, syrup, mustard, and salt in a small bowl. Whisk in olive oil, season with freshly ground pepper, and set aside.

LAST In a large bowl, toss greens, pears, and figs with enough dressing to coat. Divide between 4 plates, top with walnuts, and serve.

FROM MY KITCHEN *This salad easily adapts to suit the season and whatever you have on hand. Try apples instead of pears, or top with Manchego or blue cheese.*

Spinach Salad
with Strawberries and Blue Cheese

This basic vinaigrette works with almost any combination of vegetables, fruits, and cheeses, so you can tailor the salad to include whatever ingredients are in season.

PREP TIME 15 minutes
YIELDS 6 servings

Dressing

3 tablespoons red wine vinegar
1 small shallot, minced
Juice of ½ lemon
1 teaspoon Dijon mustard
½ cup olive oil

Salad

5 ounces (8 cups) baby spinach
1 ½ cups fresh strawberries, hulled, cut lengthwise into thick slices
3 ounces good-quality blue cheese, cut into thin slices
¼ cup thinly sliced almonds, lightly toasted

FIRST Combine vinegar, minced shallot, lemon juice, and mustard in a small bowl. Slowly whisk in olive oil, season with salt and pepper, and set aside.

LAST In a large bowl, combine spinach and strawberries. Toss with enough dressing to coat lightly. Arrange greens on salad plates, top with blue cheese slices, and sprinkle with almonds.

Green Jacket Salad

If my mom served salad with supper, it was always this recipe, which came from the old Green Jacket restaurant in Macon, Georgia. I learned recently that the original version appears in the classic *Tea-Time at the Masters* cookbook.

PREP TIME 10 minutes
COOK TIME 8 minutes
YIELDS 4-6 servings

Salad

1   pita, split in half
2   teaspoons olive oil
¼   cup plus 2 tablespoons finely grated
    Parmesan cheese
1 ¼ cups cherry tomatoes, halved
3   tablespoons thinly sliced scallions
2   tablespoons chopped flat-leaf parsley
8   cups assorted mixed greens

Dressing

2   tablespoons red wine vinegar
½   teaspoon dried oregano
¼   teaspoon salt
¼   teaspoon sugar
3   tablespoons olive oil

FIRST Preheat oven to 350°F. Place pita halves, cut side up, on baking sheet. Drizzle with olive oil and sprinkle with 2 tablespoons cheese. Bake for 8 minutes or until lightly toasted. After pitas have cooled, break into bite-size pieces and set aside.

NEXT Meanwhile, in a small bowl, whisk together dressing ingredients, season with pepper, and set aside.

LAST Combine tomatoes, scallions, and parsley in a large salad bowl. Drizzle with 3 tablespoons dressing and gently toss to coat. Allow to marinate for 5 minutes. Toss with greens, ¼ cup cheese, and pita chips as well as additional dressing, if needed.

Five Easy Salad Dressings

Homemade salad dressings are so effortless, and so flavorful, that store-bought brands aren't worth the fridge space. Just combine the ingredients in a jar, give it a few vigorous shakes, and voila—you'll have fresh dressing handy when you're in a rush.

1. Buttermilk and Chive Dressing

(yields ⅔ cup)

Add ¼ cup blue cheese crumbles, if you like, to turn this into another old-fashioned favorite.

¼ cup plus 1 tablespoon Greek yogurt
¼ cup low-fat buttermilk
1 tablespoon minced shallot
½ tablespoon white wine or champagne vinegar
½ tablespoon chopped fresh chives

Whisk ingredients together and season with salt and freshly cracked black pepper.

PERFECT PARTNERS
- *Arugula, tomatoes, Kalamata olives, and hearts of palm*
- *Roasted beets, spinach, and walnuts*
- *Grilled salmon, green beans, and steamed new potatoes over spinach*
- *Romaine lettuce, creamy blue cheese, tomatoes, and crumbled bacon*

2. Lemon Dijon Vinaigrette

(yields ½ cup)

2 tablespoons fresh lemon juice
2 teaspoons lemon zest
2 teaspoons Dijon mustard
½ teaspoon sugar
¼ teaspoon salt
6 tablespoons olive oil

Whisk together lemon juice, zest, mustard, sugar, and salt. Slowly add olive oil, whisking until emulsified and smooth. Season with freshly ground black pepper.

PERFECT PARTNERS
- *Finely sliced green apples, fennel, mint, and Parmesan cheese*
- *Roasted green beans, currants, almonds, and goat cheese*
- *Baby romaine hearts, avocado, oranges, fresh basil, and crabmeat*

(Salad dressings continued on the next page)

(Salad dressings continued)

3. Strawberry Vinaigrette
(yields 1 cup)

¾ cup fresh strawberries, hulled and sliced
2   tablespoons champagne or white wine vinegar
1 ½ tablespoons honey
1   tablespoon lime juice
½   teaspoon lime zest
1   small shallot, roughly chopped
¼   cup olive oil

Combine strawberries, vinegar, honey, lime juice, zest, and shallot in a blender or food processor and process until smooth. With motor running, slowly add oil; season with salt and pepper and refrigerate until ready to serve.

PERFECT PARTNERS
- *Bibb lettuce, radishes, and walnuts*
- *Spinach, green beans, and goat cheese*
- *Watercress and avocado*

4. Poppy Seed Dressing
(yields ¾ cup)

¼   cup minced sweet onion
2   tablespoons sugar
½   tablespoon honey
2   teaspoons poppy seeds
1   teaspoon sesame seeds
1   teaspoon Dijon mustard
¼   teaspoon salt
⅛   teaspoon paprika
¼   cup unseasoned rice wine vinegar
¼   cup canola oil

Whisk together ingredients and season with freshly cracked black pepper to taste.

PERFECT PARTNERS
- *Spinach and strawberry salad with fresh goat cheese or feta*
- *Mandarin oranges and avocado over mixed greens*
- *Nectarines or peaches with walnuts and goat cheese*

5. Balsamic Vinaigrette
(yields ½ cup)

2   tablespoons balsamic vinegar
2   teaspoons Dijon mustard
2   teaspoons minced shallot
¼   teaspoon salt
2   tablespoons fresh herbs such as basil, thyme, or tarragon (optional)
6   tablespoons olive oil

Whisk vinegar, mustard, shallot, salt, and herbs. Slowly add olive oil, whisking until emulsified and smooth. Season with freshly ground black pepper.

PERFECT PARTNERS
- *Mixed greens, cherries, pistachios, and goat cheese*
- *Grilled vegetables and Parmesan curls*
- *Roasted asparagus, cherry tomatoes, spinach, and blue cheese*

Basil Oil

Basil thrives in the Southern heat, and every summer I have a bumper crop outside my door. I make batches of this oil throughout the season to drizzle on grilled vegetables, toss with tomatoes, or whisk into salad dressings.

PREP TIME 10 minutes, plus chill time
COOK TIME 1 minute
YIELDS 1 cup

1 bunch fresh basil
   (leaves and stems intact)
½ cup olive oil
½ cup vegetable oil

FIRST Bring a large pot of water to a boil. Submerge basil in water for 5 seconds, remove, and transfer immediately to an ice bath.

NEXT Remove basil from water, squeeze out liquid, and pat dry. Process basil in a food processor or blender with olive oil. Slowly add vegetable oil and blend until smooth, about 1 minute. Refrigerate overnight.

LAST Bring oil to room temperature. Line a mesh strainer with two layers of cheesecloth and strain oil into a bowl, discarding solids. Refrigerate oil in a glass jar for up to 2 weeks.

Buddy Ward & Son's Seafood

APALACHICOLA, FL Just ask the locals: One taste of an oyster fresh out of Apalachicola Bay, and you'll be hooked by its uniquely robust yet gentle flavor. Apalachicola's fishing industry supplies about a tenth of U.S. oysters along with boatloads of shrimp, crab, and more. Among the area's legends is Buddy Ward and Son's, run by the Ward family for more than half a century, and known for some of the best seafood in the region as well as for their longtime commitment to keeping their industry and community vital.

Left: The "Rodney and Candy," which has been shrimping for Buddy Ward and Son's for 30 years, is docked alongside the warehouse in downtown Apalachicola. Above left: A worker bags and weighs just-harvested oysters before they're shipped for sale under the company's 13 Mile Brand.

The seafood industry, which has been treasured and honored by generations of locals, is a point of pride in Apalachicola, known for some of the best-quality fish and shellfish in the country.

LUNCH

Healthy Tarragon Chicken Salad

Artichoke Rice Salad

Traditional Egg Salad

Pimenna Cheese (Pimento Cheese)

Tomato Aspic

Tomato Cracker Salad

Marinated Turkey

Roasted Chicken, Potato, and Arugula Salad
with Blue Cheese Vinaigrette

Country Ham, Mozzarella, and Arugula Sandwiches

Marinated Cucumbers and Tomatoes

Homemade Mayonnaise

Healthy Tarragon Chicken Salad

This is my favorite go-to lunch. It tastes like traditional chicken salad, with a nice crunch from the pecans and gentle sweetness from the tarragon—but thanks to a blend of light mayonnaise and plain yogurt, this recipe is much better for you than most. It is perfect for stuffing into pitas or between slices of whole-grain bread.

PREP TIME 15 minutes
COOK TIME 35 minutes
YIELDS 6 servings

3 pounds bone-in, skin-on chicken breasts
1 tablespoon olive oil
1 cup chopped celery
3 tablespoons toasted and chopped pecans

Dressing

¼ cup light mayonnaise
¼ cup plain yogurt
1 tablespoon lemon juice
1 teaspoon Dijon mustard
3 tablespoons fresh tarragon, roughly chopped

FIRST Preheat oven to 375°F. Place chicken on a parchment-lined baking pan, drizzle with olive oil, and season with salt and pepper. Bake for 35 minutes or until internal temperature registers 165°F on a meat thermometer. Once chicken has cooled, remove skin and meat from bones and chop into chunks (you should have about 3 cups).

NEXT In a large bowl, combine mayonnaise, yogurt, lemon juice, mustard, and tarragon.

LAST Add chicken, celery, and pecans to dressing ingredients. Combine well and season with salt and pepper to taste.

Artichoke Rice Salad
with Bulgur Wheat

I don't think I've ever been to a potluck church lunch that didn't have an artichoke-and-rice salad on the buffet. It's traditionally made with yellow rice and lots of mayonnaise; this version uses healthy whole grains and is every bit as delicious.

PREP TIME 10 minutes
COOK TIME 20 minutes
YIELDS 6 servings

1   cup bulgur wheat
4   tablespoons regular or
    light mayonnaise
½   teaspoon curry powder
1   (6-ounce) jar marinated artichoke hearts,
    drained, 2 tablespoons marinade reserved
½   cup chopped orange bell pepper
½   cup thinly sliced scallions
½   cup sliced green olives
1   tablespoon chopped flat-leaf parsley

FIRST Bring 2 cups water to a boil in a medium pot. Add bulgur wheat, cover, and remove from heat. Let soak for 20 minutes or until almost all water is absorbed.

LAST Combine mayonnaise and curry powder in a large mixing bowl. Drain bulgur of any excess water and add to bowl along with artichoke hearts, bell pepper, scallions, olives, and parsley. Mix well, stirring in reserved artichoke marinade. Season to taste with salt and pepper. Serve at room temperature or chilled.

Traditional Egg Salad

Since we keep chickens in our backyard, we always have more eggs than we need. This salad is one of my favorite ways to use them. I generally add more egg whites than yolks to lighten it up and stir in either chopped green olives or fresh tarragon, depending on my mood.

PREP TIME 10 minutes
COOK TIME 12 minutes
YIELDS enough for 2 sandwiches

6 eggs
2 tablespoons light mayonnaise
1 teaspoon Dijon mustard
¼ cup chopped celery
2 tablespoons chopped green olives with pimentos or 1 tablespoon fresh tarragon, chopped

FIRST Place eggs in a large stockpot in a single layer. Add enough cold water to cover the eggs by an inch. Bring to a boil; cover pot and remove from heat. Let stand 10 minutes. Drain and run cool water over the eggs. Allow to cool.

NEXT Peel eggs and cut in half. Reserve 3 egg yolks for another use. Roughly chop eggs and place in mixing bowl.

LAST Stir in mayonnaise, mustard, celery, and olives or tarragon. Season with salt and pepper and serve with mixed greens or on a sandwich (add freshly sliced tomatoes and bacon, if you like).

Pimenna Cheese (Pimento Cheese)

No Southern picnic is complete without good old "pimenna cheese." When I was growing up, my mom always kept a batch in the fridge for last-minute snacking.

PREP TIME 10 minutes
YIELDS about 2 cups

10 ounces good-quality sharp
    cheddar cheese
1 (4-ounce) jar diced pimentos, undrained
½ cup homemade or store-bought Southern
    mayonnaise, such as Duke's
1 tablespoon finely minced sweet onion
½ teaspoon Worcestershire sauce
Cayenne pepper to taste

FIRST Using a hand grater or a food processor with cheese-shredding attachment, shred cheese into a large bowl.

NEXT Add pimentos with juice, mayonnaise, onion, and Worcestershire; combine well. Season to taste with salt, black pepper, and cayenne pepper.

LAST Refrigerate until ready to serve. Spread on a sandwich or serve with saltine crackers or celery sticks.

FROM MY KITCHEN *Where I come from, "Duke's" is synonymous with "mayonnaise"—it's the closest thing you'll find to homemade. If you're counting calories, Duke's Light is just as good as the original.*

Tomato Aspic

While I was not much on congealed salads growing up, I do love tomato aspic. It's not unlike gazpacho, and just as refreshing. We always put green olives in our version—they add a pleasing saltiness and textural interest.

PREP TIME 15 minutes, plus chill time
YIELDS 10 servings

½ cup boiling water
2 envelopes unflavored gelatin
4 cups tomato juice, preferably organic
½ cup finely chopped celery
½ cup chopped pimento-stuffed green olives
¼ cup grated sweet onion
3 tablespoons sherry vinegar
1 ½ tablespoons Worcestershire sauce
½ teaspoon Tabasco sauce
½ teaspoon salt
1 tablespoon chopped fresh basil
Mayonnaise to serve (optional)

Special equipment: ring mold or bundt pan

FIRST In a large bowl, pour boiling water over gelatin and whisk until dissolved. Stir in tomato juice, celery, olives, onion, vinegar, Worcestershire, Tabasco, salt, and basil.

LAST Pour into a lightly oiled ring mold, cover with plastic wrap, and chill until set. Serve with mayonnaise, if desired.

Tomato Cracker Salad

Although a lot of my friends have never had this salad, my mom made it almost daily during the summer, when tomatoes were at their juicy best. As my daddy always says, "It is so good it will make you slap your grandmama down!"

PREP TIME 10 minutes
YIELDS 6 servings

2   medium ripe tomatoes, roughly chopped
2   hard-boiled eggs, cut in large chunks
½   medium sweet onion, such as Vidalia,
     thinly sliced
¼   cup plus 2 tablespoons mayonnaise
     (light or regular)
½   sleeve saltine crackers (about 20 crackers)

FIRST   Place tomatoes, eggs, onion, and mayonnaise in a medium bowl. Season with salt and freshly ground pepper.

LAST   Using hands, gently crush crackers into large chunks; add to bowl. Stir until all ingredients are lightly coated with mayonnaise. Serve immediately.

Marinated Turkey

We always serve this for the Masters Golf Tournament, and it's the first thing guests devour. The marinade adds a tangy flavor, similar to vinegar-based barbecue sauce, and makes the meat so tender that it falls right off the bone.

PREP TIME 10 minutes
COOK TIME 4-5 hours
YIELDS 18 servings

Marinade

1   cup apple cider vinegar
¼   cup chopped flat-leaf parsley
⅛   cup vegetable or canola oil
⅛   cup freshly ground black pepper
⅛   cup kosher salt

1   (5- to 6-pound) turkey breast

Special equipment: 1 turkey-roasting oven bag

FIRST Preheat oven to 300°F. Combine vinegar, parsley, oil, pepper, and salt in a small bowl. Place turkey in oven bag and set in a shallow roasting pan. Pour marinade over turkey in bag, seal, and bake 4 hours for a 5-pound breast (5 hours for a 6-pound breast).

NEXT Remove pan from oven and let turkey cool in bag. Remove turkey, pour juices into large measuring cup, and refrigerate. Using hands, shred turkey meat and discard bones.

LAST Once reserved marinade has cooled, skim fat from top, drizzle over turkey, and serve.

FROM MY KITCHEN *When we have weekend houseguests, I make a big batch of this for quick lunches. It's always gone by Sunday night.*

Roasted Chicken, Potato, and Arugula Salad
with Blue Cheese Vinaigrette

A friend of mine calls this the best salad ever. It's hard to disagree—who can resist so many appealing flavors in a single dish? I like it as a light lunch or supper on hot days, but omit the chicken and it becomes a lovely side.

PREP TIME 15 minutes
COOK TIME 20 minutes
YIELDS 6 servings

Salad

2   pounds Yukon Gold potatoes, unpeeled, cut into ½-inch cubes
2   cups shredded roast chicken
3   cups baby arugula
1   cup cherry tomatoes, halved
1 ½   tablespoons finely chopped fresh chives
3   slices bacon, cooked

Vinaigrette

3   tablespoons red wine vinegar
Juice of ½ lemon
¼   cup olive oil
⅓   cup crumbled blue cheese

FIRST Place potatoes in a large pot and cover with salted water by 2 inches. Simmer potatoes, uncovered, until tender, about 15 to 20 minutes. Drain and let cool.

NEXT While potatoes cook, prepare dressing. Whisk together vinegar, lemon juice, and oil in a small bowl. Stir in cheese and season with salt and pepper. Set aside.

LAST Toss potatoes with chicken, arugula, tomatoes, chives, and enough dressing to coat. Crumble bacon on top and serve.

Country Ham, Mozzarella, and Arugula Sandwiches

Think of this as a Southern take on Italian panini. With a big bowl of butternut squash soup on the side, nothing beats it for lunch on a fall afternoon.

PREP TIME 10 minutes
COOK TIME 12 minutes
YIELDS 4 servings

8 thick slices good-quality sandwich bread
Olive oil for brushing
8 ounces fresh, water-packed mozzarella cheese, cut into slices
8 ounces thinly sliced country ham or prosciutto
1 cup baby arugula
1 tablespoon good-quality balsamic vinegar
Freshly cracked pepper

FIRST Lightly brush one side of each bread slice with olive oil. Place slices, oiled sides down, on cutting board. Divide half of cheese slices among 4 slices of bread. Layer ham and arugula on top, drizzle with vinegar, and season with freshly cracked pepper. Divide remaining cheese slices among sandwiches and top each with 1 remaining bread slice, oiled side up.

LAST Heat a large skillet, preferably cast iron, over medium heat. Place sandwiches in skillet, working in batches if needed. Toast sandwiches for 6 minutes per side, pressing with a spatula to flatten, until bread is golden brown and cheese is melted.

Marinated Cucumbers and Tomatoes

Very light, very refreshing, this salad is popular all over the South in hot weather. It's easy to tweak based on what you have handy—my mom used to make it with just cucumbers and onions if there were no tomatoes in the house.

PREP TIME 10 minutes, plus marinating time
YIELDS 6-8 servings

Dressing

4 tablespoons olive oil
3 tablespoons white wine vinegar
½ teaspoon kosher salt
½ teaspoon sugar

Salad

2 medium ripe tomatoes, cut into wedges
1 large cucumber, peeled, seeded, and cut into ¼-inch slices
1 medium Vidalia or other sweet onion, cut in half and thinly sliced

FIRST In a small bowl, whisk dressing ingredients together and set aside.

LAST Gently toss tomatoes, cucumber, and onion together in a large bowl. Drizzle with dressing, season with freshly cracked black pepper, and toss to coat. Marinate for 30 minutes at room temperature or in refrigerator before serving.

Homemade Mayonnaise

If you've never had homemade mayonnaise, you're in for something special—store-bought versions can't compare. I add a little olive oil for an extra-vibrant flavor, but you can use all canola oil. With homegrown tomatoes and fresh bread, it's a little piece of heaven!

PREP TIME 10 minutes
YIELDS about ¾ cup

1   egg yolk
1 ½ teaspoons lemon juice
1   teaspoon white wine vinegar
1   teaspoon Dijon mustard
¼ teaspoon salt
½ cup canola oil
¼ cup olive oil

FIRST Whisk together egg yolk, lemon juice, vinegar, mustard, and salt in a large mixing bowl. Very slowly, drizzle oil in a steady stream into egg mixture, whisking constantly, until mayonnaise is thick, about 8 minutes. Refrigerate for up to 2 days.

White Oak Pastures

BLUFFTON, GA For more than a decade, Will Harris of White Oak Pastures—family-run since the 1860s—has been dedicated to raising all-natural grass-fed beef that's locally produced. Cattle on his farm are allowed to roam and graze freely, nourished by their mothers' milk and local hay and grasses. The result: beef that's healthier and better-tasting than that raised by more conventional methods, and a sustainable operation that preserves the tradition of respect for the Georgia countryside.

*Left: Harris holds an iron bearing the brand (now retired) that his great-grandfather created in 1866. Because branding is considered inhumane, White Oak Pastures has discontinued the practice. **Above:** Since the farm's inception, every generation of female cows has been born on the property.*

Harris checks on and cares for livestock in the fields. He and his team at White Oak Pastures are committed to producing healthful, top-quality beef and to good stewardship of the land and local resources.

SUPPER

Shrimp Burgers with Homemade Tartar Sauce

Shrimp and Artichoke Bake

Herbed Salmon with "Crowded House" Cucumber Salad

Oven-Fried Catfish with Summer Succotash

Classic Meatloaf

Country Captain Stew

Grilled Chicken with Strawberry Feta Salsa

Asian Salmon Croquettes

Summer Seafood Stew over Parmesan Grits

Balsamic Roasted Chicken and Vegetables

Sunday Roast Beef

Molasses-Glazed Pork Tenderloin

Mama's Beef Stroganoff

Grilled Bacon-Wrapped Quail

Oven-Baked Risotto with Country Ham and Peas

Roasted Trout with Okra and Black-Eyed Peas

Grilled Beef Fillets with Blue Cheese Crust

Shrimp Creole Risotto

Granddaddy's Barbecue Sauce

Shrimp Burgers
with Homemade Tartar Sauce

These decadent burgers, found at seafood dives along the coast, are the South's version of the Maryland crab cake. Don't forget the homemade tartar sauce—it's a must.

PREP TIME 25 minutes, plus chill time
COOK TIME 8 minutes
YIELDS 4 servings

Burgers

1 ½ pounds fresh shrimp, peeled
¼ cup finely chopped celery
3 tablespoons light mayonnaise
2 tablespoons finely chopped scallion
1 tablespoon chopped fresh parsley
2 teaspoons Dijon mustard
Zest of ½ lemon
½ teaspoon Old Bay seasoning
¼ teaspoon cayenne pepper
1 cup fresh bread crumbs

1 tablespoon vegetable oil
4 whole-wheat burger buns
Lettuce and sliced tomatoes
Homemade Tartar Sauce (see next page)

FIRST In a food processor, pulse shrimp until half is coarsely chopped and half is finely minced, about 8 or 9 quick pulses. Set shrimp aside.

NEXT Combine celery, mayonnaise, scallion, parsley, mustard, zest, and seasonings in a large bowl. Fold in shrimp until combined. Add bread crumbs to mixture and gently stir until well incorporated. Form mixture into 4 equal-size patties and place in a small baking pan lined with wax paper. Refrigerate for 30 minutes.

LAST In a medium skillet, preferably cast iron, heat oil over medium heat. Cook burgers for about 3 to 4 minutes per side until nicely browned, flipping only once. Serve on whole-wheat buns with lettuce, tomato, and tartar sauce.

Homemade Tartar Sauce

PREP TIME 5 minutes
YIELDS generous ½ cup

½ cup light mayonnaise
1 tablespoon sweet pickle relish
2 teaspoons capers, chopped
2 teaspoons lemon juice
½ tablespoon prepared horseradish
1 teaspoon whole-grain mustard
Tabasco sauce to taste

FIRST Combine all ingredients. Serve with shrimp burgers, crab cakes, or fried vegetables such as zucchini.

FROM MY KITCHEN *This sauce also makes a delicious topping for fish tacos and grilled or fried shrimp.*

Shrimp and Artichoke Bake

This is my version of the classic shrimp and artichoke casserole that is so popular in church cookbooks. I make it with a tomato base instead of the usual cream, and it is amazing over grits or couscous. I always use local shrimp for maximum flavor and freshness.

PREP TIME 10 minutes
COOK TIME 25 minutes
YIELDS 4 servings

1 tablespoon olive oil
1 medium onion, chopped (about 1 ½ cups)
2 large cloves garlic
1 (14.5-ounce) can fire-roasted diced tomatoes
1 (14.5-ounce) can regular diced tomatoes
1 cup marinated artichoke hearts, drained
¼ cup white wine
¼ teaspoon red pepper flakes
1 pound shrimp, peeled and deveined, tails left intact
¼ cup chopped fresh basil
¼ cup chopped fresh parsley
½ cup crumbled feta cheese

FIRST Preheat oven to 425°F. In a large skillet, sauté onion and garlic in oil over medium heat until softened and beginning to brown, about 3 to 4 minutes. Add tomatoes, artichokes, wine, and red pepper and simmer for 7 to 8 minutes until sauce has thickened.

NEXT Remove skillet from heat and stir in shrimp and fresh herbs. Season with salt and pepper to taste. Pour shrimp mixture into an 8 ½x11-inch baking dish coated with cooking spray. Sprinkle with feta.

LAST Bake for 15 minutes until shrimp are done. Serve over couscous, rice, or grits.

Herbed Salmon
with "Crowded House" Cucumber Salad

Herb-flecked salmon makes a natural partner for this crisp, refreshing salad, which is inspired by a dish from the classic Southern cookbook *Charleston Receipts*.

PREP TIME 20 minutes
COOK TIME 12 minutes
YIELDS 4 servings

Salmon

2 tablespoons finely chopped flat-leaf parsley
1 tablespoon finely chopped fresh mint
1 clove garlic, minced
2 tablespoons olive oil
4 (6-ounce) salmon fillets

Salad

¾ cup low-fat sour cream
3 tablespoons fresh lemon juice
3 tablespoons fresh mint, coarsely chopped
½ teaspoon kosher salt
Cayenne pepper to taste
3 cups very thinly sliced English cucumber (about 1 medium cucumber)

FIRST Preheat oven to 450°F. To make herb rub for salmon, combine parsley, mint, garlic, and olive oil. Season with salt and pepper and rub on top and sides of salmon. Set fish aside at room temperature while preparing salad (no longer than 20 minutes).

NEXT In a medium bowl, combine sour cream, lemon juice, mint, salt, and cayenne. Add cucumbers, toss to coat, and set aside. Line a baking sheet with foil and lightly oil. Bake salmon, skin side down, for 10 minutes or until salmon is medium-rare.

LAST Divide cucumber mixture between 4 plates and top with salmon to serve.

Oven-Fried Catfish
with Summer Succotash

Fish fries, featuring local Flint River catfish, were a regular Friday-night event in my hometown. I've lightened the classic recipe by oven-frying, and I like to serve it with succotash for a uniquely Southern twist.

PREP TIME 20 minutes
COOK TIME 12-15 minutes
YIELDS 6 servings

6 catfish fillets
2 cups buttermilk

Breading

1 teaspoon salt
1 teaspoon garlic powder
1 teaspoon onion powder
1 cup panko bread crumbs
1 cup plain cornmeal

Summer Succotash (see next page)
Lemon wedges to serve

FIRST Preheat oven to 450°F. Place catfish in a glass baking dish and pour buttermilk over fish, making sure all fillets are well coated. Let soak for 15 minutes at room temperature.

NEXT Place a cookie sheet in oven to heat. Combine breading ingredients in a 9x13-inch glass baking dish and season with salt and pepper. Coat each fillet in bread crumb mixture. Carefully grease hot cookie sheet and place fish on pan.

LAST Place cookie sheet on top rack of oven and bake for 12 to 15 minutes until fish flakes easily with fork. Serve with lemon wedges and succotash.

FROM MY KITCHEN *Panko, which are flaky Japanese-style bread crumbs, yield a remarkably light and crispy crust. They're available in Asian markets and most well-stocked supermarkets.*

Summer Succotash

I love this dish because it's light and fresh and always reminds me of hot summer days. Serve it as a cold salad or at room temperature with fish or chicken.

PREP TIME 10 minutes
COOK TIME 6 minutes
YIELDS 4-6 servings

2   cups chicken or vegetable stock
2   cups fresh or frozen butterbeans or lima beans
2   cups fresh corn, cut off the cob
2   cups cherry tomatoes, halved
2   tablespoons white wine vinegar
1   tablespoon olive oil
½   cup fresh basil leaves

FIRST Bring stock to a boil in a medium saucepan. Add butterbeans and simmer for about 4 minutes or until tender. Using a slotted spoon, remove beans and transfer to a large mixing bowl. Add corn to stock and allow to cook for 2 to 3 minutes until crisp-tender. Drain corn and transfer to bowl.

NEXT Add tomatoes, vinegar, and olive oil to bean mixture and season with salt to taste. Allow to sit at room temperature until ready to serve.

LAST Just before serving, thinly slice basil and toss with succotash to combine.

Classic Meatloaf

Down-home comfort food brings back so many memories of growing up. Meatloaf, creamy mashed potatoes, and sweet peas were regulars on our table, just like on countless others. These days, I use lean sirloin to make my meatloaf a little healthier.

PREP TIME 15 minutes
COOK TIME 1 hour
YIELDS 6 servings, plus leftovers

Meatloaf

2   pounds lean ground beef or sirloin
1   small onion, diced (about 1 cup)
½   cup tomato sauce
1   egg, lightly beaten
3   tablespoons chopped fresh parsley
1   clove garlic, minced
1   tablespoon Dijon mustard
1 ½ teaspoons dried oregano
¾   teaspoon kosher salt
¾   cup fresh bread crumbs from about
    2 slices sandwich bread

Sauce

¾   cup tomato sauce
3   tablespoons brown sugar
1 ½ tablespoons white wine vinegar
1 ½ teaspoons Worcestershire sauce

FIRST Preheat oven to 350°F. Using hands, combine meatloaf ingredients in a large bowl until well mixed. Season with freshly ground black pepper.

NEXT Using hands, shape meat into a 5x9-inch oval loaf and place in a 9x13-inch baking dish. Combine sauce ingredients in a small bowl and brush over meatloaf, reserving some for basting.

LAST Bake for about 50 to 60 minutes until internal temperature registers 155°F. Baste with sauce once or twice throughout cooking. Let rest 10 minutes before slicing. Serve with extra sauce, if desired.

Country Captain Stew

Curry-scented Country Captain, generally made with a whole cut-up chicken, is an old favorite in this region. I've substituted chunks of chicken breast to turn it into a stew that's quick enough for weeknight suppers.

PREP TIME 20 minutes
COOK TIME 35 minutes
YIELDS 4 servings

1 ½ teaspoons curry powder
¼ teaspoon salt
¼ teaspoon cayenne pepper
1 ½ tablespoons olive oil, divided
1 pound boneless, skinless chicken breasts, cut into ½-inch pieces
1 medium onion, chopped
½ yellow bell pepper, chopped
½ green bell pepper, chopped
2 cloves garlic, minced
1 (28-ounce) can whole plum tomatoes
3 cups chicken stock
¼ cup slivered almonds
1 ½ tablespoons currants

3 cups brown rice, cooked according to package directions

FIRST Combine curry powder, salt, and pepper and toss chicken in mixture to coat. Heat 2 teaspoons oil in a large stockpot over medium-high heat. Sauté chicken for 5 minutes until browned; transfer chicken to a plate and set aside.

NEXT Heat remaining oil in a stockpot over medium-high heat; add onion, peppers, and garlic and sauté for 8 minutes or until tender. Add tomatoes, breaking them up with hands or back of spoon. Add chicken and stock; season with salt to taste.

LAST Simmer soup, uncovered, for 20 minutes. Spoon rice into bowls and ladle stew over rice. Top with almonds and currants and serve.

Grilled Chicken
with Strawberry Feta Salsa

The key to this versatile salsa is choosing a fruit or vegetable that's at the peak of its season. During the hot summer months, I love using fresh peaches or watermelon; in fall and winter, roasted sweet potatoes make a perfect substitute.

PREP TIME 10 minutes
COOK TIME 25 minutes
YIELDS 4 servings

Salsa

- 2 cups fresh strawberries, hulled and quartered
- ½ cup finely chopped sweet onion
- 2 tablespoons lime juice
- ¼ cup crumbled feta cheese
- 2 teaspoons olive oil
- 1 avocado, peeled and diced

Chicken

- 1 tablespoon olive oil
- 2 teaspoons lime juice
- 4 (6- to 8-ounce) boneless, skinless chicken breast halves

FIRST In a medium bowl, combine strawberries, onion, lime juice, feta, and olive oil; set aside.

NEXT Preheat grill or grill pan to medium heat. In a large bowl, whisk together 1 tablespoon olive oil and 2 teaspoons lime juice and season with salt and pepper. Add chicken breasts and toss to coat. Grill chicken for 6 minutes per side or until meat thermometer reads 165°F. Loosely cover chicken with foil and let rest for 5 minutes.

LAST Add chopped avocado to salsa and season with salt and pepper; toss gently. Top chicken with salsa and serve.

Asian Salmon Croquettes

Quick, inexpensive, and made with pantry staples, salmon croquettes have been a Southern standby for years. While the old-fashioned recipe is delicious, I've added Asian ingredients to create an outstanding variation.

PREP TIME 15 minutes, plus chill time
COOK TIME 8 minutes
YIELDS 4 servings

1   (15-ounce) can wild salmon, skin and bones removed
½   cup finely chopped red or yellow bell pepper
2   tablespoons finely chopped scallions
2   tablespoons chopped flat-leaf parsley
2   tablespoons mayonnaise
1   tablespoon soy sauce
1   teaspoon grated fresh ginger
½   teaspoon sesame oil
1   egg
2   tablespoons lime juice
½   cup panko bread crumbs
1 to 2 tablespoons olive oil for sautéing
Lime wedges for serving

FIRST In a medium bowl, combine salmon, chopped pepper, scallions, and parsley; set aside.

NEXT Lightly whisk together mayonnaise, soy, ginger, sesame oil, egg, and lime juice in a separate bowl. Add to salmon mixture and season with pepper. Fold in bread crumbs and shape into 8 (3-inch) patties. Refrigerate patties for 20 minutes until just firm.

LAST Heat 1 to 2 tablespoons oil in a large nonstick skillet over medium-high heat. Cook croquettes, working in batches if necessary, 4 minutes per side until browned. Serve with lime wedges.

FROM MY KITCHEN *Use canned, wild sockeye salmon for this recipe—it offers the best flavor and health benefits.*

Summer Seafood Stew
over Parmesan Grits

When our family vacations on the Georgia coast during the summer, one of the things we most look forward to is making this dish. You can substitute fresh basil or other herbs for the tarragon if you choose.

PREP TIME 25 minutes
COOK TIME 30 minutes
YIELDS 4 servings

1   tablespoon olive oil
1   small fennel bulb, very thinly sliced
1   medium leek, white and light green parts only, thinly sliced
3   cloves garlic, chopped
1   cup white wine
2   pounds fresh tomatoes, chopped
1   cup clam juice
½   teaspoon kosher salt
1   pound fresh grouper, snapper, or other white fish, cut into 2-inch pieces
1   pound fresh, local shrimp, peeled
1   pound mussels, scrubbed
1   tablespoon sherry vinegar
3   tablespoons chopped fresh tarragon, divided

FIRST Prepare Parmesan Grits and allow to simmer while prepping for stew. In a large stockpot over medium-high heat, heat oil and sauté fennel, leeks, and garlic for 10 minutes until tender. Add wine, tomatoes, clam juice, and salt and lightly simmer for 5 minutes.

NEXT Add fish, cover, and cook for 2 minutes. Add shrimp and mussels, cover, and cook until shrimp are pink and mussels have opened, about 4 minutes. Stir in vinegar, 2 tablespoons tarragon, and season with salt and freshly ground black pepper to taste.

LAST Remove any mussels that are unopened. Spoon ¾ cup grits into each of 4 bowls, ladle stew over grits, and top each bowl with remaining tarragon before serving.

Parmesan Grits

2 cups water
2 cups chicken stock, preferably organic
1 cup stone-ground grits
½ cup freshly grated Parmesan cheese
½ tablespoon butter

FIRST Bring water and stock to a boil. Slowly whisk in grits. Reduce heat and simmer for 30 minutes.

LAST Stir in cheese and butter; season with salt and pepper to taste.

Balsamic Roasted Chicken and Vegetables

This robust one-dish meal pairs balsamic-kissed chicken with a colorful tumble of root vegetables—just right for autumn evenings with a little snap in the air. I like to make it in a cast-iron skillet, which distributes heat evenly and keeps the vegetables tender beneath a crispy skin.

PREP TIME 15 minutes
COOK TIME 35 minutes
YIELDS 4-6 servings

Chicken

1   whole chicken, 3 ½ to 4 pounds
½   teaspoon kosher salt
4   carrots, sliced ¾ inch thick
    (about 2 cups)
1   pound small Yukon Gold potatoes, halved
1   large onion, quartered

Balsamic Sauce

3   tablespoons balsamic vinegar
3   tablespoons chicken stock
2   tablespoons olive oil
1   tablespoon honey
1   tablespoon fresh oregano, chopped
2   teaspoons fresh rosemary, chopped

FIRST Preheat oven to 500°F. Rinse chicken with water, pat dry, and rub with ½ teaspoon kosher salt. Butterfly chicken by removing the backbone with kitchen scissors and set aside.

NEXT Place carrots, potatoes, and onion inside a 12-inch cast-iron skillet or glass baking dish (coat with cooking spray if using glass). Lay chicken on top of vegetables, breast side up, tucking wing tips. Combine sauce ingredients and pour over top of chicken.

LAST Place skillet on middle rack of oven and roast for 15 minutes. Reduce temperature to 400°F and continue cooking for an additional 15 to 20 minutes or until a meat thermometer registers 165°F in thickest part of breast. Let meat rest for 15 minutes before cutting.

> **FROM MY KITCHEN** *We Southern cooks have a longstanding love affair with cast-iron skillets—because they hold heat so well, nothing beats them for searing chops, frying chicken, or turning out cornbread with a gorgeous sheath of brown crust. If your grandmother didn't hand hers down, it's worth investing in your own. My favorite source is Lodge Cast Iron, a family-owned company that's based in the Tennessee mountains and produces some of the best cast-iron cookware you can buy.*

Sunday Roast Beef

On Sundays, Mama would often bake a roast to have for sandwiches throughout the week. She always soaked it a day ahead of time in a flavorful marinade and, after it came out of the oven, sliced the beef very thin. With a little horseradish sauce, it makes a delicious lunch.

PREP TIME 10 minutes, plus marinating time
COOK TIME 2 hours
YIELDS 8 servings

Marinade

½ cup vegetable oil
½ cup soy sauce
3 tablespoons Worcestershire sauce
¼ cup apple cider vinegar
Juice of 1 lemon
1 ½ tablespoons dry mustard
½ teaspoon salt
1 tablespoon freshly ground black pepper, plus more for coating

2- to 3-pound eye of round roast

FIRST Place roast in a deep bowl or zip-top plastic bag. Whisk together oil, soy, Worcestershire, vinegar, lemon juice, mustard, salt, and pepper. Pour over beef and marinate for at least 8 hours, turning occasionally.

NEXT Preheat oven to 500°F. Place a wire rack atop a foil-lined baking sheet. Remove roast from marinade and roll in pepper. Place roast on wire rack and cook for 5 minutes per pound. Turn oven off (do not open oven door) and continue to cook for about 1 ½ to 1 ¾ hours. A meat thermometer inserted in the thickest part of the roast should register 130°F for medium rare and 140°F for medium. If roast is not done after 1 ¾ hours, heat oven to 225°F for 5 minutes, turn off, and continue to cook until roast reaches desired temperature.

LAST Let roast rest for 15 minutes before carving. Slice very thin to serve.

Molasses-Glazed Pork Tenderloin

Sweet molasses and Dijon mustard blend in a marinade that's tasty with both pork and chicken. Be careful not to overcook the pork; it should be very tender.

PREP TIME 10 minutes, plus marinating time
COOK TIME 20 minutes
YIELDS 6 servings

Marinade

- ¼ cup unsulfured molasses
- 3 tablespoons soy sauce
- 2 tablespoons olive oil
- 1 tablespoon lemon juice
- 1 tablespoon Dijon mustard
- 1 teaspoon freshly grated ginger
- 2 cloves garlic, chopped

- 2 pork tenderloins, about ¾ pound each, trimmed and silverskin removed

FIRST Combine marinade ingredients and season with freshly ground black pepper. Place pork in a glass baking dish and pour marinade over to coat. Marinate in refrigerator for at least 1 hour and up to 3 hours, turning occasionally. Twenty minutes before cooking, remove dish from refrigerator and let stand at room temperature.

NEXT Preheat grill to medium-high heat. Remove pork from marinade; discard marinade. Grill pork, turning occasionally, until thickest part registers 140°F on an instant-read thermometer, about 18 minutes. Remove from grill, tent loosely with foil, and let meat rest for 5 minutes.

LAST Slice into 1-inch-thick slices and serve.

Mama's Beef Stroganoff

My brother, my sister, and I all loved this comfort classic growing up, and my mom made it for us every couple of weeks. It tastes rich, but lean sirloin and low-fat sour cream keep it on the lighter side.

PREP TIME 15 minutes
COOK TIME 30 minutes
YIELDS 4-6 servings

1   tablespoon olive oil
1   medium onion, cut in half and thinly sliced
2   cloves garlic, minced
12 ounces baby portobello or
     button mushrooms
1 ½ pounds sirloin steak, trimmed and
     very thinly sliced
2   tablespoons Worcestershire sauce
1 ¾ cups beef stock
2   tablespoons tomato paste
2   tablespoons flour
⅓ cup low-fat sour cream
2   tablespoons chopped flat-leaf parsley

Brown rice or egg noodles, cooked according
     to package directions

FIRST Heat oil in large skillet over medium heat. Sauté onions and garlic for 5 minutes until beginning to soften. Add mushrooms and continue to cook, stirring occasionally, for 8 minutes, until mushrooms are browned and onions have begun to caramelize. Transfer mixture to a bowl and set aside.

NEXT Return skillet to medium-high heat. Brown sirloin in Worcestershire sauce for 4 minutes or until meat is almost cooked through. Add onion mixture and stir in stock. Whisk in tomato paste, bring to a boil, reduce heat, and simmer for 10 minutes. In a separate dish, whisk flour with 3 tablespoons water. Slowly whisk mixture into pan and stir over low heat until slightly thick, about 3 to 4 minutes.

LAST Just before serving, stir in sour cream and top with parsley. Serve over brown rice or egg noodles.

> **FROM MY KITCHEN** *Freezing the steak for 30 minutes or so will allow you to slice it thin with ease.*

Grilled Bacon-Wrapped Quail

My dad is an enthusiastic quail hunter at his south Georgia farm, so the birds have always been a suppertime staple at our house, even for Christmas Eve. We traditionally serve them with cheese grits, biscuits, and my mom's Baked Apples and Bananas (page 162) for a warming fall feast.

PREP TIME 30 minutes, plus
    marinating time

COOK TIME 15 minutes

YIELDS 6 quail

Marinade

¼ cup red wine

¼ cup olive oil

2 cloves garlic, crushed

2 teaspoons chopped fresh rosemary

2 teaspoons chopped fresh sage

½ teaspoon salt

6 bone-in quail

6 slices thin-cut bacon

FIRST Combine wine, oil, garlic, herbs, and salt in a zip-top plastic bag. Season with cracked pepper and add quail. Marinate in refrigerator for 1 to 2 hours.

NEXT Preheat grill to medium-high heat. Wrap each quail in 1 slice of bacon and let sit at room temperature for 20 minutes before grilling.

LAST Grill quail, flipping only once, for 6 to 7 minutes per side or until internal temperature registers 165°F.

Oven-Baked Risotto
with Country Ham and Peas

Thick, creamy, and incredibly easy, this oven-baked version of risotto gets its rich flavor from good-quality Parmesan and smoky country ham. My favorite comes from Benton's Country Hams, right out of Tennessee.

PREP TIME 10 minutes
COOK TIME 45 minutes
YIELDS 6 servings

1   tablespoon olive oil
1   medium onion, chopped
2   cloves garlic, minced
5   ounces country ham, rinsed* and diced
1 ½ cups arborio rice
½   cup white wine
4 ½ cups chicken stock, divided
1   cup frozen spring peas
¾   cup finely grated, good-quality Parmesan cheese
2   tablespoons chopped mint

FIRST Preheat oven to 400°F. Heat oil in a skillet over medium-high heat. Sauté onion and garlic until soft, about 5 minutes. Add ham and sauté until warmed through and beginning to brown, about 3 minutes.

NEXT Place rice in a 9x13-inch casserole dish; stir in onion mixture, wine, and 4 cups stock. Cover tightly with foil and bake for 30 minutes. Spread peas over rice, replace foil, and bake for 10 more minutes.

LAST Remove risotto from oven and gently stir in additional ½ cup stock, cheese, and mint. Season with freshly cracked pepper and continue stirring until risotto is thick and creamy, about 3 to 4 minutes. Add more stock for a thinner consistency, if desired.

*Rinse ham with cold water and pat dry to remove some of the salt.

Roasted Trout
with Okra and Black-Eyed Peas

My husband is an avid fly fisherman and always comes home loaded down with fresh trout. We usually cook it as simply as possible to showcase its pure flavor, amped up with a relish that marries two iconic Southern ingredients.

PREP TIME 15 minutes
COOK TIME 25 minutes
YIELDS 4 servings

2   teaspoons olive oil
1   clove garlic, finely chopped
½   cup chopped red bell pepper
½   cup chopped Vidalia or other sweet onion
2   cups fresh okra, cut into ½-inch rounds
½   cup frozen or fresh black-eyed peas
¼   teaspoon red pepper flakes
½   cup chicken or vegetable stock
⅓   cup canned diced tomatoes with juice
3   teaspoons white wine vinegar
2   teaspoons capers
⅛   teaspoon smoked paprika

4   (6-ounce) trout fillets
1   teaspoon olive oil

FIRST In a large skillet over medium heat, sauté garlic, peppers, and onion until soft, about 3 to 4 minutes. Stir in okra, black-eyed peas, and red pepper. Add stock and tomatoes and bring to a boil. Reduce heat, cover, and simmer until okra is tender, about 7 minutes. Remove lid and continue to simmer until most of liquid has evaporated, about 3 minutes. Stir in vinegar, capers, and paprika. Season with salt and freshly ground black pepper to taste; set aside.

NEXT Preheat broiler and place rack 4 inches from heat source. Season trout with salt and pepper and place on greased baking sheet, skin side up. Brush skin with oil and broil for 7 minutes until skin has browned and fish is cooked through.

LAST Place trout on serving platter, spoon okra mixture on top, and serve.

FROM MY KITCHEN *The okra relish in this dish doubles as a wonderful appetizer. It's also great with grilled chicken or any type of grilled fish.*

Grilled Beef Fillets
with Blue Cheese Crust

At our house, Saturday night was steak night. Back then, you couldn't find blue cheese in Reynolds, Georgia, but my mom and I now love serving this dish to the family. Round it out with a side of grits and a big green salad.

PREP TIME 10 minutes
COOK TIME 15 minutes
YIELDS 4 servings

¼ cup panko bread crumbs
¼ cup crumbled blue cheese
2   teaspoons chopped fresh parsley
2   teaspoons Worcestershire sauce

4   (6-ounce) beef fillets
2   teaspoons olive oil

FIRST Preheat grill to high heat. In a small bowl, combine bread crumbs, cheese, parsley, and Worcestershire; season with freshly ground pepper and set aside. Brush steaks with oil and season with salt and pepper.

NEXT Grill steaks for 3 minutes per side until well browned on both sides. Reduce grill temperature to medium or move steaks to a cooler part of the grill. Continue cooking, flipping only once, about 6 minutes for rare. (Meat thermometer should read 125°F for rare and 130°F for medium-rare.)

LAST During the last 5 minutes of cooking, top each fillet with blue cheese mixture, pressing to make mixture stick. Grill until mixture begins to melt and brown. Let meat rest for 5 minutes before serving.

FROM MY KITCHEN *You can also pan-sear the fillets and finish them in the oven. Simply preheat the broiler, top cooked fillets with cheese mixture, and broil for 2 to 3 minutes until mixture begins to melt.*

Shrimp Creole Risotto

When I began to cook on my own, risotto was one of the first dishes I mastered (mostly because it's one of my favorite things to eat). It has a reputation for being difficult, but if you can stir, you can pull it off.

PREP TIME 15 minutes
COOK TIME 40 minutes
YIELDS 4 servings

1   pound peeled and deveined shrimp, peels reserved
1   tablespoon butter
3   cloves garlic, minced
1   medium onion, chopped (1 ½ cups)
1   green bell pepper, chopped (1 cup)
1 ¼ cups arborio rice
⅓   cup white wine
½   teaspoon salt
1   (15-ounce) can diced tomatoes with juice
1   bay leaf
¾   cup grated, good-quality Parmesan cheese, divided

FIRST Place shrimp peels in a large saucepan and add 5 cups water. Bring to a simmer and cook for 15 minutes. Strain through a sieve set over a bowl, reserving stock (about 4 cups). Discard solids. Return stock to saucepan and keep warm over low heat.

NEXT Melt butter in a large saucepan over medium heat. Sauté garlic, onion, and pepper until tender, about 5 minutes. Add rice and cook 2 minutes, stirring constantly. Add wine and salt and stir until most of liquid is absorbed. Add tomatoes and bay leaf and continue stirring until most juice is absorbed. Ladle in about 3 ½ cups stock, ½ cup at a time, stirring often, until each addition of stock is absorbed. Risotto is done when rice is creamy but grains are slightly firm in center.

LAST Stir in shrimp and cook for 5 minutes until shrimp are pink, stirring often. Remove from heat and stir in an additional ½ cup stock. Stir in ½ cup cheese. Season to taste with freshly ground pepper and top with remaining cheese to serve.

> **FROM MY KITCHEN** *If you run out of stock toward the end of making this dish, you can substitute hot water.*

Granddaddy's Barbecue Sauce

My grandfather managed to weasel this recipe from the owners of a famous, local barbecue restaurant. My mom and I make batches at a time and keep jars on hand for gifts.

PREP TIME 10 minutes
COOK TIME 2 hours
YIELDS 10 cups

4   cups apple cider vinegar
1   teaspoon garlic salt
1   teaspoon red pepper flakes
1   teaspoon black pepper
1   teaspoon celery seed
2   cups prepared mustard
4   cups organic ketchup
Juice of 2 lemons
1   cup sugar

Special equipment: 5 pint-size mason jars

FIRST In a large stockpot, combine vinegar, garlic salt, red and black pepper, and celery seed and bring to a boil. Add mustard, stirring with a whisk until smooth.

NEXT Reduce heat to low. Whisk in ketchup, lemon juice, and sugar. Cook, uncovered, over low heat for 2 hours, stirring occasionally.

LAST Ladle hot sauce into sterile mason jars; secure jar lids tightly. Once lids have sealed (listen for a popping sound), store jars in pantry until ready to use.

SIDES

Stuffed Vidalias with Bacon and Gruyère

Oven-Roasted Okra

Macaroni and Cheese with Caramelized Onions

Baked Apples and Bananas

Roasted Summer Vegetables

Spaghetti Squash with Rosemary and Parmesan

Brussels Sprouts with Lemon and Pecorino

Coconut Rice

Sweet Potato Salad

Mama Ra's Baked Beans

Flat Cornbread

Grits - A Southern Staple

Collards with Capers, Raisins, and Pine Nuts

Collards with Ginger and Soy

Sweet Corn Pudding

Sour Cream Rolls

Stuffed Vidalias
with Bacon and Gruyère

Vidalia onions, grown only in a 20-county belt of Georgia, get their signature sweetness from short winters and low-sulfur soil. They're available across the country from early spring through November; I can't think of a better dish than this to make the most of the season.

PREP TIME 20 minutes
COOK TIME 50 minutes
YIELDS 4 servings

4   Vidalia or other sweet onions
1   teaspoon olive oil
2   slices bacon, chopped
1 ½ cups chopped fresh spinach
2   teaspoons chopped fresh sage
½   teaspoon salt
1   cup fresh bread crumbs
⅔   cup shredded Gruyère cheese

FIRST Preheat oven to 400°F. Cut a ½-inch-thick slice off top of each onion and a thin slice off each bottom (just enough for onion to sit upright). Using a spoon, scoop out centers of onions, leaving outer 2 to 3 layers intact; reserve onion centers. Place onions in a glass baking dish with ½ cup water. Cover with foil and bake for 25 minutes.

NEXT Meanwhile, chop enough reserved onion to yield 1 cup. In a medium skillet, heat oil over medium heat. Add bacon and sauté for 30 seconds. Add onion and sauté for 7 minutes or until onion begins to brown. Remove from heat and stir in spinach, sage, and salt. Transfer mixture to a bowl. Stir in bread crumbs and cheese and season with pepper.

LAST Remove onions from baking dish and drain water. Reduce oven temperature to 350°F. Stuff bread crumb mixture into cavity of each onion, mounding on top. Return onions to baking dish and bake on middle rack for 20 minutes until thoroughly heated.

Oven-Roasted Okra

Just a handful of okra plants in your garden will yield more than a family can eat! This is an easy way to prepare it; roasting at a high temperature lends the flavor of fried okra without all the mess.

PREP TIME 5 minutes
COOK TIME 6 minutes
YIELDS 4 servings

1   pound fresh okra
1 ½ tablespoons good-quality olive oil
½   teaspoon kosher salt

FIRST Preheat broiler. Place rimmed baking sheet under broiler to preheat for 5 minutes.

NEXT Toss okra with olive oil and salt. Spread evenly on preheated pan and roast for 6 minutes, tossing occasionally, until okra is tender and beginning to brown.

LAST Season okra with freshly cracked pepper and additional salt if needed. Drizzle with extra olive oil if desired.

Macaroni and Cheese
with Caramelized Onions

This lighter version of mac and cheese, with a trio of flavorful cheeses and onions for added richness, is Southern comfort food you can feel good about serving to your family. Kids love it!

PREP TIME 10 minutes
COOK TIME 35 minutes
YIELDS 6 servings

2   teaspoons olive oil
1   medium onion, thinly sliced
1   tablespoon brown sugar
2   cups (8 ounces) dried elbow macaroni
2   tablespoons all-purpose flour
1 ½ cups 1 percent milk
3   ounces shredded cheddar cheese (¾ cup)
2   ounces shredded Parmesan cheese (½ cup)
2   ounces fresh goat cheese, divided
¼   teaspoon cayenne pepper

FIRST Preheat oven to 400°F. Heat oil in a skillet over medium-low heat. Add onions, sugar, and a pinch of salt. Sauté for 10 minutes or until golden brown, stirring often; set aside.

NEXT While onions are sautéing, cook macaroni according to package directions. Drain; return cooked macaroni to pot and set aside. Place flour in a large saucepan and gradually add milk, whisking until smooth. Cook over medium heat until thick (about 10 minutes), whisking often. Stir in cheddar, Parmesan, 1 ounce goat cheese, and cayenne pepper until smooth. Remove from heat and pour sauce over cooked macaroni; season with salt and freshly ground pepper.

LAST Pour macaroni into an 8x8-inch baking dish coated with cooking spray. Spread onions over top and crumble remaining goat cheese over onions. Bake for 15 minutes or until heated through.

Baked Apples and Bananas

From the time I was a toddler, every fall we'd head to a quail plantation owned by my parents' good friends, Mr. John and Mrs. Sally. To accompany her grilled quail, Mrs. Sally always made her mother's recipe for baked apples and bananas. This dish now has become a tradition in our own family; we never have a quail supper without it.

PREP TIME 15 minutes
COOK TIME 55 minutes
YIELDS 6 servings

4   bananas, cut into ½-inch slices
1   tablespoon lemon juice
3   Gala apples, peeled, cored, and cut into
     ¼-inch slices
½   teaspoon salt
3   tablespoons butter
3   tablespoons packed brown sugar, divided

Special equipment: 1 ½-quart soufflé dish

FIRST Preheat oven to 350°F. In a medium bowl, toss bananas with lemon juice. Spread ⅓ of bananas in bottom of lightly buttered dish, top with ⅓ of apples, and sprinkle with 1 tablespoon of brown sugar and a pinch of salt. Slice butter into very thin slices and place ⅓ of slices on top of fruit. Repeat steps twice more, ending with sugar and butter.

LAST Bake for 45 to 55 minutes until apples are tender. Serve with grilled quail, duck, or pork.

Roasted Summer Vegetables

Whether you have a thriving garden or a good local market, summer vegetables can pile up fast in your kitchen. This method allows you to make use of your bounty in one easy dish.

PREP TIME 15 minutes
COOK TIME 35 minutes
YIELDS 6 servings

Dressing

2   tablespoons olive oil
1   tablespoon white balsamic or white wine vinegar
½   teaspoon Dijon mustard
1   teaspoon salt
¾   teaspoon freshly ground black pepper

Vegetables

1   medium zucchini, cut into 1-inch pieces
2   medium crookneck squash, sliced into half-moons
1   medium eggplant (about 1 pound), cut into 1-inch pieces
1   orange or red bell pepper, cut into 1-inch pieces
1   medium onion, cut into 1-inch wedges
3   cloves garlic, peeled and chopped
2   tablespoons chopped fresh oregano
Small handful thyme sprigs
1 ½ cups grape or cherry tomatoes
2   ounces crumbled feta cheese
¼   cup coarsely chopped fresh basil

FIRST Preheat oven to 450°F. Whisk dressing ingredients together in a small bowl and set aside.

NEXT Combine vegetables, garlic, oregano, and thyme in a large bowl. Toss with dressing and spread vegetables in a single layer on a large, rimmed baking sheet coated with oil (use a second baking sheet if necessary).

LAST Roast in oven for 25 minutes or until almost done, stirring vegetables halfway through cooking. Toss in tomatoes, return to oven, and roast for an additional 10 minutes or until vegetables are tender and beginning to brown. Toss with feta cheese and basil before serving.

> **FROM MY KITCHEN** *To streamline prep work, don't bother stripping the leaves from thyme sprigs when you roast them with meat or vegetables. Just toss them in whole; the leaves will fall off the woody stems as they cook, and the stems are easily removed afterward.*

Spaghetti Squash
with Rosemary and Parmesan

Folks tend to forget about spaghetti squash, which is a shame. It has a wonderful, buttery flavor, and when it's baked, the texture is just like thin spaghetti. I love it tossed with a little olive oil, good cheese, and my favorite vegetables (or even fruit).

PREP TIME 10 minutes
COOK TIME 1 hour
YIELDS 4-6 servings

1   (3-pound) spaghetti squash
1½ tablespoons olive oil, divided
2   cloves garlic
1   tablespoon chopped fresh rosemary
1   teaspoon salt
1   cup red grapes, halved
2   tablespoons chopped pecans,
     lightly toasted
1   ounce Parmesan cheese, shaved with
     a vegetable peeler

FIRST Preheat oven to 375°F. Slice spaghetti squash in half lengthwise and remove seeds. Drizzle with ½ tablespoon oil and lightly sprinkle with salt and pepper. Place squash, cut side down, on a greased, rimmed baking sheet. Roast for 45 minutes or until fork-tender. Let cool for 10 minutes. Using a fork, shred squash into a bowl to resemble spaghetti.

LAST Heat remaining 1 tablespoon oil in a large skillet over medium-low heat. Sauté garlic and rosemary until fragrant, about 15 seconds; do not allow to burn. Add squash and salt and increase heat to medium. Cook squash, stirring often, about 5 minutes. Remove from heat and toss with grapes, pecans, and cheese. Season with salt and pepper to taste.

> **FROM MY KITCHEN** *I always keep a block of good-quality Parmigiano-Reggiano cheese on hand. The taste difference between the authentic version and less expensive supermarket brands is like night and day. Wrapped in parchment paper and then in tinfoil, it will keep in the fridge for weeks.*

Brussels Sprouts
with Lemon and Pecorino

Brussels sprouts, one of my favorite vegetables, often get overlooked at the market. These are shredded, which gives them a different look and texture and may even fool those non-Brussels sprout fans.

PREP TIME 15 minutes
COOK TIME 15 minutes
YIELDS 6 servings

2   pounds Brussels sprouts
2   tablespoons butter
2   medium shallots, sliced into thin rings
½   cup chicken stock
2   tablespoons lemon juice
½   cup finely shredded, good-quality Pecorino cheese
½   cup toasted, chopped walnuts

FIRST Remove outer leaves of Brussels sprouts and cut each sprout in half down center of stem. Lay sprouts on cut sides and slice crosswise into thin strips.

NEXT In a large skillet, heat butter over medium heat. Sauté shallots for 6 to 7 minutes or until caramelized. Add Brussels sprouts and cook, stirring occasionally, for an additional 3 minutes. Stir in chicken stock and continue cooking for 4 to 5 minutes until sprouts are tender.

LAST Stir in lemon juice, cheese, and nuts; season with salt and pepper to taste.

Coconut Rice

Every time my mom served cube steak, she added a helping of creamy rice on the side. She cooks hers with regular milk; I chose light coconut milk for a richer flavor. Serve this with Molasses-Glazed Pork Tenderloin (page 142) and Collards with Ginger and Soy (page 178).

PREP TIME 2 minutes
COOK TIME 15 minutes
YIELDS 4 servings

1   cup jasmine rice
1   cup water
1   cup light coconut milk
½   teaspoon salt

FIRST Place rice in a fine-mesh strainer and rinse under cold water for about 10 seconds; set aside.

NEXT Bring water and coconut milk to a boil in a medium saucepan. Add salt and rice. Reduce heat to low, cover, and cook until done, about 15 minutes.

LAST Fluff with fork and serve.

> **FROM MY KITCHEN** *In addition to its distinctive flavor, jasmine rice is fluffier and cooks faster than plain white rice.*

Sweet Potato Salad

This sweet potato salad, tossed in a light vinaigrette and studded with crunchy pecans, makes a perfect side dish to accompany barbecued or fried chicken in the summer, or with roast pork in the fall.

PREP TIME 15 minutes
COOK TIME 10 minutes
YIELDS 4-5 servings

Dressing

- 2 tablespoons sherry vinegar
- 2 tablespoons olive oil
- 2 teaspoons honey
- 1 teaspoon Dijon mustard

Salad

- 2 pounds sweet potatoes, peeled and cut into ½- to ¾-inch cubes
- 2 tablespoons dried currants or dried cranberries
- ¼ cup pecan halves, toasted and roughly chopped
- ⅛ cup very thinly sliced red onion
- 1 cup baby arugula

FIRST Whisk dressing ingredients in a small bowl to blend. Season with salt and pepper and set aside.

NEXT Bring a large pot of salted water to a boil, add potatoes, and return to a boil. Reduce heat and simmer for 6 minutes or until potatoes are fork-tender. Drain and let cool at room temperature. In a microwave-safe dish, combine currants with 3 tablespoons water and microwave for 30 seconds to rehydrate; drain.

LAST Combine potatoes, currants, pecans, and onion in a large bowl. Toss with dressing and arugula and serve.

> **FROM MY KITCHEN** *This salad can easily be made ahead and served cold or at room temperature. Toss in the arugula right before serving.*

Mama Ra's Baked Beans

My mom learned to make this family favorite from her grandmother, Mama Ra, and always served it with her juicy burgers and oven-roasted fries. I've added a variety of beans for color and texture, but it has the same delicious flavor I remember.

PREP TIME 15 minutes
COOK TIME 1 hour 20 minutes
YIELDS 6-8 servings

2   teaspoons olive oil
2   cloves garlic, minced
1   medium sweet onion, chopped
1   medium green bell pepper, chopped
1   (15-ounce) can pinto beans, rinsed
    and drained
1   (16-ounce) can chickpeas, rinsed
    and drained
1   (15-ounce) can kidney beans, rinsed
    and drained
1   cup frozen baby lima beans
2   cups tomato sauce
½   cup brown sugar
¼   cup apple cider vinegar
2   tablespoons molasses
1   teaspoon dry mustard
½   teaspoon ground ginger
½   teaspoon red pepper flakes
3   slices good-quality bacon

FIRST Preheat oven to 350°F. Heat oil in a large skillet over medium-high heat. Sauté garlic, onion, and bell pepper for 5 minutes or until softened.

NEXT Combine onion mixture, beans, tomato sauce, sugar, vinegar, molasses, mustard, ginger, and red pepper in a large bowl. Pour into a greased 9x13-inch baking dish and place bacon slices across top.

LAST Cover dish with tinfoil and bake for 30 minutes. Remove foil and bake for an additional 25 minutes.

Flat Cornbread

Deep-dish cornbread was the norm at our house, but when Mama served us vegetable beef soup, her "flat cornbread," as I called it, was always on the side. These little cakes are terrific when you're short on time but crave something warm and comforting. And if you have leftovers, you can do what I did as a child: crumble them into a glass of buttermilk and call it dessert!

PREP TIME 5 minutes
COOK TIME 15 minutes
YIELDS about 14 cakes

1   cup self-rising cornmeal
1 ¼ cups buttermilk
2   tablespoons vegetable oil, divided

FIRST Combine cornmeal and buttermilk in a mixing bowl. Heat 1 tablespoon oil in a large cast-iron skillet over medium heat.

LAST Ladle 2 tablespoons of batter to form each cake, cooking 2 to 3 at a time. Cook for 1 minute per side until cornbread is brown and cooked through. Use remaining oil to grease skillet for each new batch. Transfer cakes to a baking pan and place in a 200°F oven to keep warm while preparing remaining batches. Serve with a pat of butter, if desired.

Grits – A Southern Staple

Mention Southern cooking, and nine times out of ten, grits are the first thing that pops into people's minds. Incredibly versatile, they're equally at home on the breakfast table or as a side dish at supper. They're also a blank canvas for flavorful stir-ins—my suggestions below are just a starting point.

Basic Grits:

PREP TIME 5 minutes
COOK TIME 50 minutes
YIELDS 4 servings

4   cups water
1   teaspoon salt
1   cup stone-ground grits
1   tablespoon butter (optional)

FIRST Bring water to a boil in a medium saucepan. Add salt and whisk in grits slowly so that no clumps form. Reduce to a simmer and cook for about 50 minutes, until grits are creamy and tender. Add a small amount of additional water if needed.

LAST Stir in cheese, butter, or desired additions (below). Season with salt and freshly ground pepper and serve.

> **FROM MY KITCHEN** *I prefer stone-ground grits for their texture and pure corn flavor, and because they are better for you. You can also substitute organic chicken stock for about half the water to boost the taste.*

GRITS AND GREENS: Add 2 ounces shredded white cheddar cheese and ½ cup cooked, chopped spinach or collard greens.

CREAMY GRITS: Stir in ½ cup mascarpone cheese.

SMOKY GRITS: Add 2 ounces smoked cheddar cheese and a pinch or two of cayenne pepper.

CORN GRITS: Stir in 1 cup fresh, cooked corn kernels, cut off the cob, and 1 tablespoon chopped fresh basil.

PARMESAN GRITS: Add ½ cup finely grated Parmesan cheese (perfect for shrimp and grits or with Summer Seafood Stew, p. 137).

WILD MUSHROOM GRITS: Stir in 1 cup sautéed wild mushrooms and ¼ cup Parmesan or goat cheese.

Collards
with Capers, Raisins, and Pine Nuts

While I am not a fan of traditional collard greens cooked with fatback (which is exactly what I grew up on), I do love to dress collards up with flavors from around the globe. This Italian-influenced version—studded with capers, pine nuts and golden raisins—is a sassy, sophisticated take on a Southern standby.

PREP TIME 15 minutes
COOK TIME 10 minutes
YIELDS 4-6 servings

2   teaspoons olive oil
¼   cup finely chopped shallots
1 ¼   pounds collard greens, ribs and stalks removed and leaves sliced crosswise into ribbons (about 15 cups of greens)
½   cup chicken or vegetable stock
½   teaspoon salt
2   tablespoons golden raisins
1 ½   tablespoons balsamic vinegar
1 ½   tablespoons toasted pine nuts
1   tablespoon capers

FIRST Heat oil in a large stockpot over medium heat. Add shallots and sauté until tender, about 3 minutes. Add half of greens, stock, and salt and cook until greens wilt slightly, about 3 minutes. Using tongs, fold in remaining greens so that wilted greens are mostly on top.

NEXT Add raisins, cover pot with lid, and reduce heat to low. Cook for 8 to 10 minutes until greens are tender, tossing occasionally.

LAST Toss greens with vinegar and season with pepper. Arrange on platter and top with pine nuts and capers; drizzle with extra olive oil, if desired.

> **FROM MY KITCHEN** *During the fall and winter months, many stores sell large bags of pre-cut collards, which make these recipes a snap. You can easily substitute any type of winter greens, or try a combination of kale, mustard greens, collards, and turnip greens.*

Collards
with Ginger and Soy

I gravitate to Asian-inspired recipes such as this one, a wonderful blend of salty, sweet, and spicy flavors. Even people who have never liked collards have become huge fans of this dish.

PREP TIME 5 minutes
COOK TIME 15 minutes
YIELDS 4-6 servings

3   cloves garlic, minced
1 ¼ pounds collard greens, ribs and stalks removed and leaves sliced crosswise into ribbons (about 15 cups of greens)
1   teaspoon salt
½   cup chicken or vegetable stock
¼   cup hoisin sauce
3   tablespoons soy sauce
1   teaspoon finely grated fresh gingerroot
1 ½ teaspoons sesame oil
½   teaspoon red pepper flakes
½   cup sliced water chestnuts
Sesame seeds (optional)

FIRST Heat oil in a large saucepan over medium heat. Sauté garlic until fragrant, about 30 seconds. Add half of collards and salt and stir until slightly wilted. Add remaining collards and stock and sauté for 5 minutes.

NEXT Cover saucepan with lid, reduce heat, and cook for 10 minutes, stirring occasionally, until greens are tender. Season with salt and pepper to taste.

LAST While greens are cooking, combine hoisin sauce, soy, ginger, sesame oil, and red pepper in a small bowl. Stir into cooked collards until well combined. To serve, place greens on a platter; top with water chestnuts and sesame seeds, if desired.

Sweet Corn Pudding

This pudding is best when made with the freshest possible sweet corn (I'm partial to Silver Queen). The just-picked flavor really stands out.

PREP TIME 15 minutes
COOK TIME 1 hour 10 minutes
YIELDS 6 servings

2   tablespoons butter
3   tablespoons all-purpose flour
3   cups milk
3   eggs
1   teaspoon salt
3   cups fresh corn kernels, cut from cob
    (about 6 ears)

FIRST Preheat oven to 400°F. In a medium saucepan, melt butter over medium heat and stir in flour. Add milk, whisking constantly, and continue cooking until thickened and smooth, about 5 minutes.

NEXT In a medium bowl, beat eggs until frothy. Slowly whisk in about 1 cup of hot milk mixture. Slowly whisk egg mixture into remaining milk mixture on stovetop and cook about 1 minute, stirring constantly (do not boil). Remove from heat, stir in salt and corn, and season with freshly ground pepper.

LAST Pour corn mixture into a greased 2-quart baking dish. Place dish into a 3-quart baking dish and place on middle rack of oven. Carefully pour enough hot water into larger dish to come halfway up sides of smaller dish. Bake 1 hour, uncovered, until pudding is just set.

Sour Cream Rolls

These rolls are delicious straight out of the oven. Growing up, we never sat down to Sunday lunch without a basket full of them on our table.

PREP TIME 5 minutes
COOK TIME 15 minutes
YIELDS about 30 rolls

½ cup (1 stick) butter, melted
8 ounces sour cream
2 cups self-rising flour

Special equipment: mini muffin tins

FIRST Preheat oven to 425°F. In a medium bowl, stir together butter, sour cream, and flour. Drop by heaping tablespoons into greased mini muffin tins.

LAST Bake for 15 minutes or until rolls begin to brown; serve immediately.

Sweet Georgia Peaches

GEORGIA IS FAMOUS FOR ITS PEACHES. For those who grow them, they're a labor of love that pays off in unparalleled flavor. I was lucky enough to grow up in the heart of the peach belt, just down the road from the four largest farms. Dickey Farms, Georgia's oldest, still operates at the same site along the railroad from which they once transported sweet peaches up north. I spent a number of summers selling peaches and pecans at Lane Southern Orchards, and my parents' best friends own the largest family-owned farm in the state, Taylor Orchards.

Lawton Pearson, a dear childhood friend, runs Pearson Farm with his dad in Fort Valley. According to him, the region's soil, heat, and humidity all have a hand in that signature Georgia peach sweetness. And when they're sold close to home, he says, "We can pick them at the last possible minute, which means they have enough time to get all the sugar in them." What better testament to the rewards of buying local?

Above: A worker at Lane Southern Orchards oversees the bins in which peach-pickers place the fruit that is pulled from the trees.

Phillip Rigdon (bottom row, center) of Lane Southern Orchards and Lawton Pearson (bottom row, right) of Pearson Farm both have taken active roles in their families' peach businesses. Although growing peaches is challenging and inherently risky, Pearson says, the sense of accomplishment at the end of the season is well worth it.

At local packing sheds (Taylor Orchards and Pearson Farm are pictured above), peaches are weighed individually by automated cups, then sorted by weight and hand-graded into three categories: No. 1, No. 2, or No. 3. The No. 1 peaches are those that get shipped to grocery stores across the country.

DESSERTS

Strawberry Basil Buttermilk Sorbet

Hummingbird Cupcakes

Milk Flips

Bourbon Peach Bread Pudding
with White Chocolate Sauce

Buckeyes

Mint Julep Chocolate Sauce

Blackberry Crumble

Mrs. Dull's Ice Box Cookies

Fresh Berry and Cream Cheese Tart
with Pecan Shortbread Crust

Dot's Butterscotch Brownies

Cornmeal Peach Cake

Thumbprint Cookies

Gingersnap Ice Cream Sandwiches

Key Lime Parfaits

Kentucky Derby Pie

Strawberry Basil Buttermilk Sorbet

This sorbet showcases spring strawberries at their best. The buttermilk gives it a rich flavor that's reminiscent of ice cream—a refreshing end to a big meal.

PREP TIME 10 minutes, plus chill time
YIELDS 6-8 servings

2   cups fresh strawberries, hulled
2   cups low-fat buttermilk
4 to 5 fresh basil leaves
1   cup sugar
1   teaspoon vanilla
Fresh basil or mint to garnish

Special equipment: 1 ½-quart electric ice
    cream maker

FIRST Process strawberries in a food processor or blender until smooth. Pour puree through a wire-mesh strainer into a large bowl, pressing with back of spoon. Discard solids and set puree aside.

NEXT Add buttermilk and basil to blender and puree until basil is finely chopped. Add buttermilk mixture to strawberry puree and whisk in sugar and vanilla. Cover and chill for at least 1 hour.

LAST Pour mixture into freezer container of a 1 ½-quart electric ice cream maker. Freeze according to manufacturer's instructions. Scoop into bowls and garnish with mint or basil, if desired.

Hummingbird Cupcakes

My maternal grandmother, Mama Chess, adores hummingbird cake, and my mom bakes one for her birthday every year. The trick to keeping it light and fluffy is to stir the batter with a wooden spoon instead of a mixer. I like to make it into cupcakes so I can give them away and dodge the temptation of an entire cake sitting on my sideboard.

PREP TIME 30 minutes
COOK TIME 30 minutes
YIELDS 26 cupcakes

2   cups all-purpose flour
2   cups sugar
1 ½   teaspoons ground cinnamon
1   teaspoon baking soda
1   teaspoon salt
3   eggs
1 ½   cups canola oil
2   cups mashed ripe bananas
1   (8-ounce) can crushed pineapple with juice
1   teaspoon vanilla
1 ½   cups pecans or walnuts, toasted and chopped

FIRST Preheat oven to 350°F. Line standard-size muffin tins with paper liners. Combine flour, sugar, cinnamon, soda, and salt in a bowl and set aside.

NEXT In a large bowl, beat eggs with a wire whisk. Using a wooden spoon, stir in oil, bananas, pineapple, and vanilla. Gradually add flour mixture and stir until well combined. Fold in pecans.

LAST Divide batter evenly among lined cups, filling each to about ½ inch below the top. Bake for 28 to 30 minutes or until a cake tester inserted in center comes out clean and tops are lightly browned. Once cooled, spread with Orange Cream Cheese Icing and store in refrigerator until ready to serve.

Orange Cream Cheese Icing

1   (8-ounce) package Neufchatel cheese, softened
¼   cup (½ stick) butter, softened
2   teaspoons fresh orange juice
½   teaspoon fresh orange zest
4   cups (1 pound) powdered sugar

FIRST Using an electric mixer, cream together cheese and butter. Beat in orange juice and zest. Slowly add sugar and beat until smooth and creamy.

Milk Flips

On Christmas Day, my family usually gathered at the home of our close friends Mr. Garland and Mrs. Gloria, where the men would all toast the holiday with milk flips. Of course, their version was much stronger than mine—adjust the brandy as you see fit.

PREP TIME 10 minutes
YIELDS 4 servings

½ cup brandy, or more to taste
½ cup milk
3 tablespoons sugar
1 teaspoon vanilla
1 pint vanilla ice cream
Grated nutmeg

FIRST Combine brandy, milk, sugar, vanilla, and ice cream in a blender and process until smooth.

LAST Divide evenly among cups and top with grated nutmeg to serve.

Bourbon Peach Bread Pudding
with White Chocolate Sauce

This is one of my favorite ways to use fresh Georgia peaches. Laced with bourbon and drizzled with white chocolate sauce, it's over-the-top good.

PREP TIME 20 minutes, plus chill time
COOK TIME 55 minutes
YIELDS 9 servings

Pudding

1 ¼ cups 1 percent milk

1 (12-ounce) can evaporated skim milk

¾ cup brown sugar

¼ cup bourbon

1 tablespoon vanilla

¼ teaspoon nutmeg

¼ teaspoon cinnamon

3 eggs, lightly beaten

2 ½ cups peeled, chopped fresh peaches (with juice)

8 cups (1-inch cubes) good-quality white bread (not sandwich bread)

Sauce

⅓ cup sugar

2 tablespoons butter

1 cup 1 percent milk

1 tablespoon cornstarch

2 tablespoons white chocolate chips

1 teaspoon vanilla

FIRST In a large bowl, whisk together milk, evaporated milk, sugar, bourbon, vanilla, spices, and eggs. Add peaches and bread and toss to combine. Cover and chill for 1 hour.

NEXT Preheat oven to 350°F. Spoon bread mixture into a lightly oiled 11x8-inch baking dish. Bake for 50 minutes until set.

LAST To prepare sauce, melt sugar and butter in a medium saucepan over medium heat. In a separate bowl, whisk together milk and cornstarch. Add milk mixture to saucepan and bring to a boil. Reduce heat, stir in white chocolate and vanilla, and cook until sauce is smooth and thickened, about 2 to 3 minutes. Cut pudding into 9 squares, plate, and drizzle sauce over each serving.

Buckeyes

A Southern Christmas tradition, these little chocolate and peanut butter candies are sinful. They resemble the shiny nuts from the buckeye tree, which, as the saying goes, will bring you good luck if you carry them around in your pocket.

PREP TIME 35 minutes, plus chill time
COOK TIME 10 minutes
YIELDS about 7 ½ dozen

18 ounces crunchy peanut butter
   (not all-natural)
1 cup (2 sticks) butter, softened
1 teaspoon vanilla
4 ½ cups powdered sugar
2 cups semisweet chocolate chips
6 tablespoons half-and-half

FIRST Using an electric mixer, cream together peanut butter, butter, and vanilla until smooth. Add powdered sugar, ½ cup at a time, until well blended.

NEXT Roll dough between palms to form 1-inch balls (if dough gets too soft, chill for 10 minutes). Place on baking sheets and chill for 20 minutes or until firm.

LAST Heat chocolate and half-and-half in a heatproof bowl set over a pan of simmering water, stirring until chocolate is melted and smooth. Using a toothpick, dip each peanut butter ball into chocolate until partially coated. Place on a baking sheet lined with wax paper. Using finger, smooth peanut butter to cover toothpick hole. Refrigerate until set. Store in an airtight container.

Mint Julep Chocolate Sauce

Mint julep cocktails—practically synonymous with the South—inspired this luscious, bourbon-spiked chocolate concoction. Pour it over vanilla ice cream for a dessert that's as easy as it is elegant.

PREP TIME 10 minutes
COOK TIME 5 minutes
YIELDS 2 cups

8 ounces good-quality semisweet chocolate, chopped
1 cup heavy cream
¼ cup fresh mint leaves
½ cup light corn syrup
1 ½ tablespoons bourbon

FIRST Place chocolate in a medium bowl and set aside. Bring cream and mint leaves to a very light simmer in a medium saucepan. Cook, stirring often, for 5 minutes. Pour cream through a fine-mesh strainer set over a bowl. Discard mint.

NEXT Return cream to pot, add corn syrup, and reheat. Pour mixture over chocolate and stir until chocolate melts.

LAST Stir in bourbon and serve sauce over vanilla ice cream.

Blackberry Crumble

The dirt road across from my childhood home was lined with wild blackberry bushes, and I was always impatient for them to ripen around mid-July. After we spent a day picking them, Mama would whip up a fresh blackberry dessert for us to enjoy.

PREP TIME 15 minutes
COOK TIME 35 minutes
YIELDS 4 servings

4   cups blackberries
2   tablespoons sugar
1   tablespoon lemon juice

Crumble

¼   cup all-purpose flour
¼   cup old-fashioned rolled oats
¼   cup packed brown sugar
½   teaspoon cinnamon
3   tablespoons butter, slightly softened, plus more for greasing ramekins

Vanilla ice cream to serve

Special equipment: 4 (6-ounce) ramekins or a 9-inch pie dish

FIRST Preheat oven to 375°F. In a large bowl, combine blackberries, sugar, and lemon juice. Divide evenly among buttered ramekins or spoon into buttered pie dish.

NEXT Set dishes on rimmed baking sheet and bake for 15 minutes.

LAST Meanwhile, place flour, oats, sugar, cinnamon, and butter in a large bowl. Using fingers, mix until well combined and crumbly. Sprinkle evenly over fruit and bake until crust begins to brown, about 15 minutes. Let cool for 10 minutes before serving. Serve with vanilla ice cream.

Mrs. Dull's Ice Box Cookies

A dear friend always brags about her grandmother's ice box cookies. The original recipe came from Mrs. S.R. Dull's iconic book *Southern Cooking*, with one important tweak: These are baked in small coin-like shapes, all too easy to pop in your mouth.

PREP TIME 30 minutes
COOK TIME 10 minutes
YIELDS about 60 cookies

1 ¾ cups all-purpose flour
¼ teaspoon salt
½ teaspoon baking soda
1 stick (½ cup) butter, softened
1 cup brown sugar
1 egg
1 teaspoon vanilla
½ cup chopped pecans (optional)

FIRST Preheat oven to 350°F. Sift flour, salt, and baking soda into a medium bowl and set aside. With an electric mixer, cream together butter and sugar until light and fluffy.

NEXT Add egg and vanilla; beat until combined, scraping down sides of bowl as needed. Gradually add flour mixture, beating until just combined. Mix in nuts, if desired.

LAST Roll dough between palms to form 1-inch balls. Place 2 inches apart on a parchment-lined baking sheet and bake for 8 to 10 minutes until lightly browned. Cool cookies on wire rack.

Fresh Berry and Cream Cheese Tart
with Pecan Shortbread Crust

During the summer, my mom would make a similar version of this tart. The pecan shortbread crust complements the creamy filling perfectly. Top with whatever fresh fruit is in season, such as peaches, berries, nectarines, or figs.

PREP TIME 25 minutes, plus chill time
COOK TIME 30 minutes
YIELDS 8 servings

Crust

½ cup (1 stick) unsalted butter, chilled
½ cup sugar
1 cup all-purpose flour
½ teaspoon salt
⅓ cup pecans, finely chopped

Filling

1 cup heavy cream
1 (8-ounce) package Neufchatel or regular cream cheese, softened
2 ½ cups powdered sugar
1 teaspoon vanilla
1 ½ cups assorted fresh berries or other fruit

Special equipment: 9-inch tart pan with removable bottom

FIRST With an electric mixer on low speed, beat butter and sugar until combined. Add flour and salt and beat until well incorporated. Sprinkle in pecans and beat until blended, about 1 minute. Preheat oven to 325°F. Press dough into a 9-inch tart pan with removable bottom, pressing up sides so dough is flush with rim of pan. Chill dough for 30 minutes. Bake tart shell until it begins to brown, about 30 minutes, pressing with bottom of a glass to flatten as needed. Place on wire rack to cool in pan.

NEXT While crust is baking, beat cream on medium speed until soft peaks form; set aside. Beat cream cheese, sugar, and vanilla until fluffy; fold in whipped cream.

LAST Spread filling into prepared tart shell (you will have some filling left over). Top with assorted berries or fruit and refrigerate until slightly firm, about 30 minutes. Remove sides of pan from tart and serve.

Dot's Butterscotch Brownies

My husband's Grandmother Dot was an elegant Southern lady and a wonderful cook. She dressed to the nines and had something delightful in the oven at all times. These are a family favorite.

PREP TIME 10 minutes
COOK TIME 45 minutes
YIELDS 28 (2-inch) squares

2 cups all-purpose flour
2 teaspoons baking powder
1 teaspoon salt
1 pound light brown sugar
¾ cup (1 ½ sticks) butter
2 eggs
1 teaspoon vanilla
¾ cup pecans, chopped
¾ cup semisweet chocolate chips
    (optional)

FIRST Preheat oven to 350°F. Sift together flour, baking powder, and salt into a bowl and set aside.

NEXT Stir sugar and butter in a large saucepan over low heat until melted. Remove from heat and let cool slightly. Whisk in eggs and vanilla. Transfer to a large mixing bowl and stir in flour mixture, ½ cup at a time. Fold in pecans and chocolate chips (if using) and pour into a greased 8 ½x11-inch baking dish.

LAST Bake for 40 to 45 minutes until tester inserted in center comes out with a little gooey batter attached. Let cool and cut into 2-inch squares.

Cornmeal Peach Cake

Not overly sweet, but absolutely delicious, this cake is best served with fresh whipped cream or ice cream. The cornmeal lends a rich golden hue.

PREP TIME 25 minutes
COOK TIME 55 minutes
YIELDS 12 servings

2 ½ cups all-purpose flour
½ cup yellow cornmeal
1 tablespoon baking powder
1 teaspoon salt
4 eggs
2 cups sugar
1 cup canola or vegetable oil
¼ cup fresh orange juice
2 ½ teaspoons vanilla
3 fresh peaches, peeled and sliced
    (about 2 cups)
¼ cup sugar
1 ½ teaspoons cinnamon

Special equipment: 10-cup bundt pan

FIRST Preheat oven to 350°F. Butter and flour a 10-cup bundt pan. In a medium bowl, combine flour, cornmeal, baking powder, and salt; set aside.

NEXT Using an electric mixer with a paddle attachment or a hand mixer, beat eggs, sugar, and oil until smooth. Slowly beat in orange juice. One cup at a time, add flour mixture until incorporated. Stir in vanilla. In a medium bowl, toss peaches, sugar, and cinnamon.

LAST Pour half of batter into bundt pan, top with peaches, and finish with remaining batter. Bake for 55 minutes. Let cool in pan on wire rack for 15 minutes. Remove from pan, place on wire rack, and let cool completely.

> **FROM MY KITCHEN** *For a super-moist cake, you can add an additional cup of peaches and bake a few minutes longer. The cake may not have a neat, uniform shape, but I love the gooey center.*

Thumbprint Cookies

My mom's best friend and catering partner, Mrs. Jane, has influenced my cooking almost as much as my family has. When I was growing up, she had a plate of these buttery cookies waiting for me every time I arrived at her front door.

PREP TIME 30 minutes
COOK TIME 12 minutes
YIELDS about 22 cookies

2   cups all-purpose flour
1 ½ teaspoons baking powder
½   teaspoon salt
1   cup (2 sticks) unsalted butter, softened, plus more for greasing pans
4   tablespoons powdered sugar
1   tablespoon vanilla
1   cup finely chopped pecans (optional)
½   cup good-quality fruit preserves

FIRST Preheat oven to 375°F. Lightly grease 2 cookie sheets with butter.

NEXT Combine flour, baking powder, and salt in a large bowl and set aside. With an electric mixer on medium-high speed, cream butter and sugar until fluffy. Reduce speed to low and slowly add dry ingredients until well incorporated. Add vanilla and pecans, if using.

LAST Using hands, roll dough into 1- or 1 ½-inch balls and place on cookie sheets. Press thumb into each cookie to form a shallow well. Spoon 1 teaspoon preserves into center of each cookie. Bake for 10 to 12 minutes or until lightly browned. Let cool for 5 minutes on cookie sheets. Using a metal spatula, remove cookies and place on wire rack to cool to room temperature.

Gingersnap Ice Cream Sandwiches

Nothing against traditional ice cream sandwiches, but I like to shake things up a little. In my version, freshly made gingersnap cookies stand in for the usual chocolate wafer cookies—a homey twist that's a hit with kids and adults alike.

PREP TIME 25 minutes
COOK TIME 14 minutes
YIELDS about 20 sandwiches

2   cups all-purpose flour
1   teaspoon baking soda
2   teaspoons ginger
1   teaspoon cinnamon
¾   teaspoon salt
¼   teaspoon allspice
⅛   teaspoon white pepper
½   cup (1 stick) unsalted butter, softened
½   cup sugar, plus more for coating cookies
½   cup light brown sugar, packed
1   egg
⅓   cup unsulfured molasses

2   quarts vanilla ice cream, slightly softened

FIRST Preheat oven to 350°F. In a large bowl, combine flour, baking soda, ginger, cinnamon, salt, allspice, and white pepper. Cream butter, sugar, and brown sugar in work bowl of an electric mixer until fluffy. Add egg and molasses; beat well. With mixer set on low, spoon in flour mixture and mix until a soft dough forms.

NEXT Lightly butter hands (to prevent sticking) and form dough into 1 ¼-inch balls. Roll in sugar until coated. Place cookies on a baking sheet lined with parchment paper, about 2 inches apart. Bake for 12 to 14 minutes, until cookies have crispy edges but are still soft inside (they will be cracked in the middle). Let cool on cookie sheet for 5 minutes. Using a metal spatula, transfer to wire racks to cool to room temperature.

LAST Spoon a small scoop of vanilla ice cream onto one cookie, top with a second cookie, and press to sandwich together. Use a spreading knife to smooth edges of ice cream. Repeat until all cookies have been used. Place sandwiches on baking sheet and freeze until firm. Wrap each sandwich in plastic wrap and store in freezer until ready to serve.

Key Lime Parfaits

Key lime pie goes hand in hand with hot summer nights. I love serving this individual version when I entertain; they're so sweet that a few bites are all you need.

PREP TIME 25 minutes, plus chill time
COOK TIME 6 minutes
YIELDS 6 servings

½ cup graham cracker crumbs
1 ½ tablespoons melted butter
4 egg yolks
1 (14-ounce) can sweetened condensed milk
½ cup Key lime juice (about 8 to 10 Key limes)
4 egg whites
Pinch cream of tartar
2 tablespoons sugar

Special equipment: 6 (5-ounce) ramekins

FIRST Combine cracker crumbs and butter in a small bowl. Divide evenly among ramekins and press into bottom of each. Set aside. In a large bowl, whisk egg yolks and gradually add condensed milk, whisking until mixture is smooth. Stir in lime juice and divide mixture evenly among ramekins.

NEXT Using a stand mixer or handheld mixer, whip egg whites and cream of tartar until soft peaks form. Gradually add sugar and whip until stiff peaks form. Spoon meringue onto each parfait, mounding on top.

LAST Place ramekins on a rimmed baking sheet and bake for 5 to 6 minutes, until meringue begins to brown. Once cool enough to handle, refrigerate, uncovered, for 3 hours or until set.

> **FROM MY KITCHEN** *You can make this recipe even speedier by spreading the lime curd into purchased graham cracker tart shells. Fresh Key limes can sometimes be hard to come by, but bottles of Key lime juice are available in most supermarkets.*

Kentucky Derby Pie

My childhood friend Anne's mom is a Lexington, Kentucky native. If I was lucky, she'd be pulling this classic pie out of the oven when I came over to visit. I'm a chocolate-lover, so it's one of my favorites to make.

PREP TIME 25 minutes
COOK TIME 50 minutes
YIELDS 8 servings

Flaky Pie Crust

- 2 cups all-purpose flour
- 2 tablespoons sugar
- ½ teaspoon salt
- 12 tablespoons unsalted butter, chilled and cut into 1-inch cubes
- 3 tablespoons ice water (or more)

Pie

- ½ cup (1 stick) unsalted butter, softened
- 1 cup sugar
- 2 eggs, lightly beaten
- ½ cup flour
- ⅛ teaspoon salt
- 2 tablespoons bourbon
- 1 cup chopped pecans
- 1 cup semisweet chocolate chips

Whipped cream or ice cream to serve

Special equipment: 9-inch pie dish

FIRST In a food processor fitted with blade attachment, blend flour, sugar, and salt (if working by hand, use a pastry blender). Add butter and pulse until mixture resembles coarse meal. Add water, 1 tablespoon at a time, and process until large clumps form. Add additional water if dough appears too dry. Gather dough into a ball, roll into a ¾-inch disk, and chill for 30 minutes. Dough can be frozen for up to 3 months.

NEXT Preheat oven to 350°F. Roll dough on floured surface into a round large enough to fit into a 9-inch pie dish, with additional for overhang. Fold overhang under and crimp edges. Using a fork, lightly prick bottom of crust and bake for 15 to 20 minutes until crust begins to brown. Halfway through cooking, pierce crust with fork again to prevent bubbling (or bake with pie weights). Remove from oven and let cool.

LAST Using a mixer, cream butter and sugar together. Add eggs, flour, salt, and bourbon. Fold in pecans and chocolate chips, pour in pie shell, and bake for 35 minutes until center is set. Serve with whipped cream or ice cream.

Nora Mill Granary

HELEN, GA Tommy Martin, longtime miller at Nora Mill Granary, thinks of himself as a "grits counselor" for those who shy away from the most iconic of Southern staples. "We have people who didn't even know that grits are corn," he says, explaining that Nora Mill's method of stone grinding preserves the corn's flavor—and wholesomeness—in a way that conventional roller grinding can't. Owned by the Fain family for generations, the granary takes pride in turning out traditional corn and wheat products that are as healthful as they are delicious.

Left: Old-fashioned, stone-ground grits, bursting with pure corn flavor, are one of Nora Mill Granary's signature products. Above: Though it's been updated and refurbished to keep it running smoothly, the original structure still looks much as it did when it was built in the 19th century.

*Left: Traditional millstones are the heart of Nora Mill Granary's approach to grinding. **This page, bottom left:** Tommy Martin, who for years has served as miller at the granary, enjoys sharing with visitors the flavor and health advantages of stone-ground grits and grains.*

BREAKFAST

Herb and Goat Cheese Scrambled Eggs

Homemade Biscuits

Rosemary Biscuits with Honey Ham

Homemade Granola

Frog in the Hole with Bacon Grits

Breakfast Muesli with Dried Cherries and Vanilla

Saturday Morning Cinnamon Rolls

Nu-Way's "Mama's Special"

Apple and Sage Turkey Sausage

Fig Preserves

Herb and Goat Cheese Scrambled Eggs

I love serving this beautiful spring and summer dish over toasted ciabatta bread, with freshly squeezed orange juice on the side. Use farm-fresh eggs if you can—their vivid gold color and rich flavor will amaze you.

PREP TIME 10 minutes
COOK TIME 2 minutes
YIELDS 4 servings

Salsa

1   cup red and yellow grape tomatoes, halved
1 ½   tablespoons roughly chopped fresh basil
2   teaspoons white balsamic vinegar
2   teaspoons olive oil

Eggs

8   fresh eggs
½   cup milk
1   teaspoon chopped fresh thyme
1   teaspoon chopped fresh chives
1   teaspoon chopped flat-leaf parsley
½   teaspoon salt
½   tablespoon butter
3   ounces goat cheese, crumbled

FIRST Combine tomatoes, basil, vinegar, and oil in a medium bowl. Season with salt and freshly cracked pepper and set aside.

NEXT In a large bowl, whisk eggs, milk, herbs, and salt. Place butter in a nonstick skillet over high heat, tilting pan to coat as butter melts. Add eggs and, with a wooden spoon, slowly push from side to side, folding over as they cook. After 1 minute, sprinkle with crumbled goat cheese and fold to combine, forming a mound in center of skillet. Eggs should take about 1 ½ to 2 minutes total to cook and should still appear slightly shiny.

LAST Spoon salsa over eggs, top with freshly cracked pepper, and serve immediately.

Homemade Biscuits

My mom is known for her biscuits. Guests at our farm never wake up without a fresh batch waiting for them, ready to pile on a plate alongside country ham and grits. Doused with cane syrup, they were my favorite childhood breakfast treat.

PREP TIME 15 minutes
COOK TIME 12 minutes
YIELDS about 10 biscuits

2   cups self-rising flour, preferably White Lily
⅓ cup shortening, plus more for greasing pan
About ¾ cup buttermilk

Special equipment: 2 ½- to 3-inch
    biscuit cutter

FIRST Preheat oven to 500°F and grease a cookie sheet with shortening. Sift flour into a large bowl. Using a pastry cutter or the back of a fork, cut shortening into flour until it resembles small peas. Slowly pour enough buttermilk into flour mixture to make a sticky dough and lightly stir with a fork until dough comes away from the sides of the bowl. (You may not use all the buttermilk.)

NEXT Place dough on floured work surface and carefully roll a couple of times until coated with flour (do not handle too much or biscuits will be flat). Gently press dough to a 1- or 1 ½-inch thickness. Flour a 2 ½- to 3-inch biscuit cutter or the rim of a small drinking glass, and cut out biscuits. Lightly knead the remaining dough and repeat until all dough has been used. Place biscuits on greased cookie sheet, with edges touching (this will ensure soft biscuits).

LAST Bake for about 12 minutes until lightly browned.

FROM MY KITCHEN *To save time, I like to prepare a big batch of biscuits, cook them until almost brown, and freeze them. If you go this route, you can pop them in the oven frozen to finish cooking—they make a perfect Saturday morning breakfast on the go.*

Rosemary Biscuits
with Honey Ham

A touch of fresh rosemary and honey-coated ham punch up traditional breakfast biscuits—a no-fail appetizer or cocktail-party nibble. My mom used to serve these when she catered, and they were always a favorite with guests.

PREP TIME 15 minutes
COOK TIME 20 minutes
YIELDS about 14 biscuits

Honey Ham

2 tablespoons honey
1 ½ tablespoons brown sugar
1 ½ tablespoons prepared mustard
½ pound good-quality, thinly sliced ham

Biscuits

2 cups self-rising flour, preferably White Lily
⅓ cup shortening, plus more for greasing pan
2 teaspoons chopped fresh rosemary
1 cup buttermilk

Special equipment: 2-inch biscuit cutter

FIRST Preheat oven to 500°F and grease a cookie sheet with shortening. In a medium bowl, combine honey, brown sugar, and mustard. Roughly chop ham and toss until coated with honey mixture. Place ham in an oven-safe dish, cover with foil, and set aside.

NEXT Sift flour into a large bowl. Using a pastry cutter or the back of a fork, cut shortening into flour until it resembles small peas. Stir in rosemary. Slowly pour enough buttermilk into flour mixture to make a sticky dough and lightly stir with a fork until dough comes away from the sides of the bowl. (You may not use all the buttermilk.) Place dough on floured work surface and carefully roll a couple of times until coated with flour (do not handle too much or biscuits will be flat). Gently press dough to a 1-inch thickness. Flour a 2-inch biscuit cutter and cut out biscuits. Gently knead the remaining dough and repeat until all dough has been used. Place biscuits on greased cookie sheet, with edges touching (this will ensure soft biscuits).

LAST Bake for 10 minutes until lightly browned. Heat ham in oven until warm, about 8 minutes. Split biscuits and fill each with ham, or serve biscuits with ham on the side.

Homemade Granola

At our farm, it's a tradition to make our own cane syrup the day after Thanksgiving. Working alongside Mr. Edward, who helps my dad on the farm, we start boiling sugarcane juice early in the morning and let it reduce for hours. The syrup is not bottled until around suppertime, but the rich flavor—which highlights this granola—is worth the wait.

PREP TIME 15 minutes
COOK TIME 1 hour 10 minutes
YIELDS about 5 cups

3   cups old-fashioned rolled oats
1   cup wheat germ
1   cup pecan halves
1   cup unsweetened coconut
½   cup sunflower seeds
⅓   cup sesame seeds
½   cup cane syrup
½   cup brown sugar
¼   cup vegetable oil
½   teaspoon salt
1   cup golden raisins

FIRST Preheat oven to 250°F. In a large bowl, combine rolled oats, wheat germ, pecans, coconut, and seeds; set aside.

NEXT Whisk together syrup, sugar, oil, and salt in a small bowl. Pour over dry ingredients and toss to coat. Spread in a single layer on a greased, rimmed baking sheet.

LAST Bake until evenly browned, about 1 hour 10 minutes, stirring occasionally. Once granola has cooled, stir in raisins. Store in an airtight container.

> **FROM MY KITCHEN** *If you can't find cane syrup in your area, pure maple syrup is a good substitute.*

Frog in the Hole
with Bacon Grits

I always loved it when my mom made Frog in the Hole for me on Saturday mornings. Grits on the side were a given, but for the longest time I would only eat them if she stirred in crumbled bacon and extra butter.

PREP TIME 15 minutes
COOK TIME 50 minutes
YIELDS 2 servings

Bacon Grits

2   cups water
½   teaspoon salt
½   cup stone-ground grits
2   slices bacon, cooked
½   tablespoon butter

Frog in the Hole

2   (½-inch-thick) slices good-quality
    whole-grain bread
4   teaspoons butter, divided
2   eggs
½   teaspoon salt

Oven-roasted tomatoes to serve (optional)

Special equipment: 2-inch biscuit cutter

FIRST Bring water to a boil in a medium saucepan. Add salt and whisk in grits slowly so that no clumps form. Reduce to a simmer and cook for about 40 minutes, until grits are creamy and tender. Add a small amount of additional water if needed.

NEXT Crumble bacon into grits, add butter, and season with additional salt and freshly ground black pepper. Keep warm while preparing eggs and toast.

LAST Cut a hole into each slice of bread using a 2-inch biscuit cutter. Melt 2 teaspoons butter in a skillet over medium heat and cook 1 bread slice until golden brown, about 2 to 3 minutes. Flip bread slice and crack 1 egg into hole. Sprinkle with salt and pepper and cook for about 2 minutes or until bottom of egg is set. Using a spatula, carefully flip bread and cook 1 additional minute or until egg is done to your liking. Repeat with remaining butter, bread, and egg. Serve with grits and oven-roasted tomatoes, if desired.

> **FROM MY KITCHEN** *Even off-season cherry tomatoes are delicious when roasted in the oven. Toss them with olive oil and kosher salt and roast on a parchment-lined baking pan for 10 to 12 minutes at 375°F until they begin to burst. Season with freshly ground black pepper.*

Breakfast Muesli
with Dried Cherries and Vanilla

My summer breakfast standby, muesli is easy and ideal to have on hand for guests. Simply pull it out of the fridge and serve with toast, jam, and fresh-brewed coffee.

PREP TIME 10 minutes, plus chill time
YIELDS 4 servings

1 ½ cups old-fashioned rolled oats
⅓ cup dried cherries
¼ teaspoon cinnamon
1 cup milk
½ teaspoon vanilla
2 tablespoons plain yogurt (not Greek)
1 tablespoon honey
1 Golden Delicious apple, cored and chopped
2 tablespoons slivered almonds

FIRST Combine oats, cherries, and cinnamon in a medium bowl. Stir in milk and vanilla, cover, and refrigerate for 2 hours or overnight.

NEXT Stir in yogurt and honey and gently fold in apple and almonds. Refrigerate until ready to serve.

Saturday Morning Cinnamon Rolls

During the holidays, Mama would make batch after batch of her delicious cinnamon rolls to give as gifts. Occasionally I still make them from scratch, but to save time, I often start with purchased, frozen bread dough. They're every bit as amazing.

PREP TIME 45 minutes
COOK TIME 25 minutes
YIELDS 20 rolls

1   loaf frozen bread dough, thawed and risen until doubled in size
4   tablespoons (½ stick) butter, melted
½   cup brown sugar
1 ½ teaspoons ground cinnamon
½   cup chopped pecans (optional)
½   cup raisins (optional)

Icing

1   cup powdered sugar
3   tablespoons evaporated milk
½   teaspoon vanilla

FIRST On a floured surface, roll dough to an 8x16-inch rectangle. Brush with half of melted butter to coat. Combine brown sugar and cinnamon in a small bowl and sprinkle over dough, leaving a ½-inch border along the top long edge. Sprinkle with pecans and raisins, if desired.

NEXT Roll dough, starting at bottom long edge, to form a log. With seam side down, cut into 20 equal slices. Grease two 9-inch cake pans and arrange rolls in pans. Cover with plastic wrap and place in a warm, draft-free area to rise until they have doubled in size, about 35 minutes.

LAST Preheat oven to 350°F. Remove plastic wrap and brush tops of rolls with remaining half of melted butter. Bake for 25 minutes or until rolls begin to brown on top. To make icing, combine sugar, milk, and vanilla and whisk until smooth. Drizzle over warm rolls and serve.

Nu-Way's "Mama's Special"

As a teenager, I couldn't get enough of this breakfast treat from Nu-Way Weiners in Fort Valley, Georgia: bacon, strawberry jam, and creamy eggs piled between toast slices. In the summertime, my friend Lauren and I would grab one of these on the way to our jobs selling peaches in the heat.

PREP TIME 10 minutes
COOK TIME 10 minutes
YIELDS 1 sandwich

2   slices sandwich bread, lightly toasted
1 ½ tablespoons good-quality strawberry jam
2   eggs
2   tablespoons milk
1   teaspoon butter
1   slice bacon, cooked
2   ounces cheddar cheese, thinly sliced

FIRST Spread jam on 1 slice of bread and set aside.

NEXT Whisk eggs and milk in a medium bowl and season with salt and freshly ground pepper. Melt 1 teaspoon butter in a medium nonstick skillet over high heat. Lightly scramble eggs until they are cooked but still appear slightly shiny, about 1 ½ minutes. Layer eggs on top of jam-topped bread slice. Top with bacon and cheese. Place remaining bread slice on top and press lightly to allow heat from eggs to melt cheese.

LAST Cut sandwich in half on the diagonal and serve.

Apple and Sage Turkey Sausage

This tried-and-true combination of flavors shines in my version of traditional breakfast sausage (and no one will guess it's healthy). Serve with homemade biscuits or a stack of fluffy pancakes.

PREP TIME 15 minutes
COOK TIME 8 minutes
YIELDS 11 patties

1   pound lean ground turkey or chicken
1   Golden Delicious apple, peeled, cored, and cut into ¼-inch dice
1   medium shallot, diced (or ¼ cup chopped onion)
2   tablespoons fresh sage, chopped
½   teaspoon kosher salt
¼   teaspoon cinnamon
Pinch cayenne pepper
2   teaspoons olive oil
Maple or cane syrup to serve (optional)

FIRST Place turkey, apple, shallots, sage, salt, cinnamon, and cayenne in a large mixing bowl. Using hands, mix until ingredients are well combined. Shape into 2 ½-inch patties, about 1 inch thick.

NEXT Heat oil in a medium skillet over medium heat. Working in batches, cook patties for 3 to 4 minutes per side until well browned and cooked through.

LAST Serve with syrup on the side, if desired.

> **FROM MY KITCHEN** *With a little advance planning, you can have these on a busy morning—just cook the patties ahead of time and reheat them in a 325°F oven.*

Fig Preserves

Every year, I scope out old homes in the country to find huge fig trees so I can make a big batch of preserves. Serve them with biscuits for breakfast, or with fresh cheeses and bread as an appetizer.

PREP TIME 10 minutes
COOK TIME 1 hour
YIELDS 10 half-pint jars

4   pounds fresh, firm, ripe figs, washed
4   pounds sugar
2   lemons, thinly sliced
1   cinnamon stick
1   teaspoon whole cloves

Special equipment: 10 half-pint jars

FIRST Alternating layers, place figs, sugar, and lemon slices in a large stockpot. Add cinnamon stick and cloves and bring to a boil. Reduce heat and simmer for 1 hour, stirring occasionally to prevent sticking.

LAST Remove pot from heat and discard cinnamon stick. Spoon hot figs into sterilized jars and twist lids on tightly. Place jars in hot water bath for 5 minutes. As the jars cool, the lids will make a popping sound as they seal. Store in a cool, dark place and refrigerate after opening.

GENA KNOX

Acknowledgements

WRITING COOKBOOKS IS HARD WORK, but the rewards more than make up for it. I feel so fortunate to have a team of the most talented people I know to help me turn my inspiration into reality. Each one has devoted his or her time and skills to create a beautiful book that reflects the food, land, and people I have grown to love.

Gill Autrey, my designer and art director, has such an eye for design and has folded every element of the book into one amazing package. His hysterical stories entertained us through every photo shoot and road trip. Thank you for having the vision to help create this book and for the dedication and effort you put into it.

The beautiful photographs were taken by Erica Dines. The book would not be what it is without your incredible talent. Thank you for capturing the people, places, and food of the South in a way that makes readers feel as if they're right there with us.

Lisa Frederick, the editor, brought the book to life. She has the ability to take my ideas and stories and put them into the most beautiful words imaginable. Thank you for helping me express my passion.

Thank you to my friends who have offered feedback and support and to my official taste testers, Fiske and Katie. Without you, what would I have done with all that leftover food?

Finally, without the support of my husband, Davis, this project would not have been possible. Your patience, kindness, and love are truly amazing. Thank you for putting up with all the photo shoots in our home, as well as my crazy schedule, while balancing life with a newborn. I am so lucky to have you in my life.

GENA
KNOX

Resources and Credits

Sweet Grass Dairy
(artisan cheese from goat's, cow's,
and sheep's milk)
Thomasville, Georgia
229-227-0752
www.sweetgrassdairy.com

Fromagerie Belle Chèvre
(fresh goat cheese)
Elkmont, AL
1-800-735-2238
www.bellechevre.com

Pearson Farm
(Georgia peaches and pecans)
Fort Valley, Georgia
888-423-7374
www.pearsonfarm.com

Taylor Orchards
(Georgia peaches and strawberries)
Reynolds, Georgia
478-847-4186
www.taylororchards.com

Lane Southern Orchards
(Florida citrus; Georgia peaches and pecans)
Fort Valley, Georgia
800-27-PEACH
www.lanesouthernorchards.com

Dickey Farms
(Georgia peaches)
Musella, Georgia
1-800-PEACH-GA
www.gapeaches.com

White Oak Pastures
(grass-fed beef)
Bluffton, Georgia
229-641-2081
www.whiteoakpastures.com

Savannah Bee Co.
(specialty honey)
Savannah, Georgia
800-955-5080
www.savannahbee.com

Nora Mill Granary
(stone-ground grits and grains)
Helen, Georgia
800-927-2375
www.noramill.com

Buddy Ward and Son's Seafood
(fresh Gulf shrimp and oysters)
13 Mile Brand
Apalachicola, Florida
850-653-8522
www.13milebrand.com

Benton's Smoky Mountain Country Hams
(country ham and bacon)
Madisonville, TN
423-442-5003
www.bentonshams.com

California Fig Advisory Board
Fresno, California
559-243-8600
www.californiafigs.com

Hawthorne House
Athens, Georgia
706-227-3560
www.hawthornehouseinc.com

The Garden Shop
Apalachicola, Florida
850-653-1777
www.gardensinc.net

Lodge Manufacturing Co.
South Pittsburg, Tennessee
(cast-iron cookware)
423-837-7181
www.lodgemfg.com

Anthropologie
1-800-309-2500
www.anthropologie.com

R. Wood Studio
Athens, Georgia
888-817-9663
www.rwoodstudio.com

Captain Gill's River Cruises
Apalachicola, Florida
850-370-0075

Index

Note: *Italicized* page numbers indicate photographs.